POEMS IN HONOR OF
AFRICAN AMERICAN HEROES
AND CIVIL RIGHTS LEADERS

POEMS IN HONOR OF AFRICAN AMERICAN HEROES AND CIVIL RIGHTS LEADERS

WHAT TODAY'S YOUTH CAN GLEAN FROM THE WISDOM OF OUR ELDERS OF YESTERYEARS TO CARVE A MORE PROMISING PATH FOR THE FUTURE AHEAD

DAVID SACCOH WRIGHT

CONTENTS

David Saccoh Wright is a seasoned professional with a rich background in international affairs and a deep commitment to global development and peace. A proud alumnus of Ohio University, David holds a Master's degree in International Affairs, a testament to his academic prowess and dedication to understanding the complexities of global diplomacy and cooperation. His career began at the United Nations Development

Programme (UNDP), where he provided invaluable support to the Assistant Administrator's office within the Operations Support Group. His expertise and potential were quickly recognized, and David transitioned to the UN Secretariat as a Dutch-funded Junior Professional Officer. In this role, he contributed significantly to the Office of the Special Coordinator for Africa and Least Developed Countries, showcasing his dedication to some of the world's most vulnerable regions.

Over two decades at the United Nations have seen David evolve into a seasoned communicator and advocate within the Department of Global Communications. His work has been pivotal in shaping the narrative around the UN's mission and values, reaching out to diverse audiences worldwide. In addition, his tenure in the Department of Political and Peacebuilding Affairs has been marked by his support for conflict prevention initiatives in Africa, reflecting his unwavering commitment to fostering stability and peace on the continent.

Currently, David serves in the United Nations Office of the Special Adviser on Africa, where his focus on peace, security, and development issues continues to make a significant impact. His work is instrumental in driving forward the UN's agenda for a more peaceful and prosperous Africa, aligning with the broader goals of sustainable development and international cooperation.

Beyond his professional endeavors, David's passion for writing and mentorship shines through. He is deeply invested in guiding the youth, offering wisdom and encouragement as they navigate the complexities of life. His efforts bring a sense of hope and direction to the next generation, empowering them to build a brighter future.

As the United Nations prepares for the Summit of the Future in September 2024, David's involvement is anticipated to be a driving force in the event's success. His experience, insights, and dedication are sure to contribute to the summit's objectives, furthering the global discourse on how we can collectively forge a path toward a more equitable and sustainable world. David Saccoh Wright's legacy is one of impactful service, thoughtful leadership, and an enduring passion for making a difference in the lives of others, particularly in the realm of international affairs and development.

INTRODUCTION AND CONTEXT

In the vast narrative of American history, the story of young black kids weaves through epochs of struggle, resilience, and unyielding determination. From the early formation of colonies in the New World, where the promise of freedom clashed with the chains of slavery, to the battlegrounds of the Revolution War, where black soldiers fought for a nation's independence they were often denied, their journey has been one of relentless perseverance amidst systemic oppression.

As the dust settled after the Civil War, the ink of emancipation had barely dried before the shadows of Jim Crow cast a dark pall over the nation. Through segregation and disenfranchisement, black communities endured, their resilience becoming a testament to the human spirit's indomitable will.

Yet, it was in the crucible of the Civil Rights Movement, amidst the fiery rhetoric of leaders like Martin Luther King Jr. and the courageous marchers at Selma, that the voice of justice roared defiantly against the forces of discrimination. The hard-fought victories of voting rights seemed to promise a new dawn of equality, but the struggle was far from over.

In the wake of progress, insidious currents of inequality continued to erode the fabric of black communities. Draconian policies, pushed by political agendas, sought to strip away the hard-won rights of black citizens, leaving them vulnerable to the merciless tides of socio-economic hardship.

The emergence of the welfare system, coupled with the scourge of drugs, ravaged black inner-city neighborhoods, leaving fractured families in their wake. Fathers found themselves ensnared in the jaws of incarceration, leaving behind a generation of children to navigate the treacherous waters of life without paternal guidance.

In this landscape of adversity, black youth often find themselves at a crossroads, their dreams shackled by the harsh realities of systemic injustice. The legacy of slavery, Jim Crow, and institutionalized racism cast a long shadow over their aspirations, while the specter of police brutality looms ominously, ready to extinguish their hopes with indiscriminate violence.

For many young black boys and girls, the pursuit of success becomes a perilous journey fraught with obstacles at every turn. In a society that too often measures their worth by the color of their skin, they seek solace in avenues deemed acceptable by a prejudiced world—sports arenas or stages where their talents offer fleeting glimpses of liberation.

Yet, even these avenues are fraught with danger, as the allure of fame and fortune often leads to tragic ends. The cycle perpetuates—a vicious whirlwind of struggle and strife, where progress remains an elusive dream, and the specter of systemic injustice looms large.

In the midst of the trials and tribulations faced by young black kids in America, there emerge beacons of hope—artists whose lyrical prowess and musical talent transcend barriers and offer glimpses of a brighter tomorrow. Figures like Aubrey Graham and Kendrick Lamar have risen from the ashes of adversity, their voices resonating across generations, speaking to the struggles and triumphs of black youth.

Yet, even in the spotlight of success, the shadows of ego and rivalry loom large. Rap battles, once a hallmark of artistic expression, now carry deadly consequences if left unchecked. It is imperative for the few black leaders, both within the industry and beyond, to step forward and quell the flames of aimless conflict, guiding the next generation towards paths of collaboration and solidarity.

It is within this context that this collection of poems is crafted—not merely as a reflection of despair, but as a beacon of hope for young black youth. Through the words penned on these pages, they are invited to journey through the annals of history, to bear witness to the struggles and triumphs of those who came before. From the shackles of slavery to the battlefields of civil rights, the echoes of resilience and defiance resonate, reminding us all that freedom is not merely a gift but a hard-fought victory.

As we navigate the complexities of modern society, let us heed the wisdom of our forebears. Let us remember the sacrifices made and the battles won, and let us draw strength from their legacy as we forge ahead. For it is in unity and solidarity that the seeds of change are sown, and it is through art and expression that we find solace and inspiration.

So, to the young black youth of today, I extend an invitation—to delve into these poems not as mere words on a page, but as echoes of a collective struggle and a testament to the enduring spirit of a people. Let us reclaim our narrative, let us rewrite our story, and let us march forward with courage and conviction, knowing that the journey toward equality and justice is one we undertake together.

BOOK OF POEMS

Crispus Attucks (c. 1723 – March 5, 1770) is widely recognized as the first casualty of the Boston Massacre and, thus, the first American killed in the American Revolution. Born to an African father and a Native American mother, Attucks was a sailor and dockworker. His death symbolized the fight against British oppression and has been celebrated as a pivotal moment in American history. Though not much is known about his early life, Attucks became a symbol of black resistance and sacrifice for freedom and justice. His role in the Boston Massacre galvanized colonial sentiment against British rule, and his legacy has been honored in numerous ways, including through monuments, schools, and other public commemorations. Despite his personal achievements being less documented, Attuck's ultimate sacrifice is viewed as a significant contribution to the struggle for American independence and the broader fight for black justice and equality.

In the annals of history, bold and grand,
Stands Crispus Attucks, a patriot in this land.
In Boston's fray, he met his fate,
A symbol of courage, early and great.

Before the banners of freedom unfurled,
He stood for justice in a divided world.
In seventeen seventy, amidst the uproar and clatter,
He fell as the first in the Boston Massacre.

Now picture Crispus, if he were around,
In today's world, what might be found?
Perhaps he'd be leading, with a fervent call,
Inspiring movements, standing tall.
Would he join the marches, with banners high?
Or speak on stages, to the open sky?
Maybe he'd write, with a pen as his sword,
Crafting words of change, in every chord.

To men of today, his message rings clear,
Emulate his courage, hold it dear.
In every trial, in every fight,
Stand strong, stand tall, with all your might.

For Crispus Attucks, the pioneer,
Urges us forward, without fear.
To make our mark, to lift our voice,
And in our freedom, let us rejoice!

Salem Poor (1747 – 1802) was an African American patriot who distinguished himself during the American Revolutionary War, particularly at the Battle of Bunker Hill on June 17, 1775. Born into slavery in Andover, Massachusetts, Poor purchased his freedom in 1769 for 27 pounds, a significant sum at the time. Poor's military service is most notable for his actions at Bunker Hill, where he was credited with the heroics that earned him commendation from 14 officers, who petitioned the General Court of Massachusetts in December 1775, praising his bravery and character. This recognition was rare for African Americans during that period and highlighted his contribution to the Patriot cause. Although detailed records of his life are sparse, Salem Poor's legacy endures as an example of the critical role

African Americans played in the fight for American independence. His bravery and the formal recognition he received underscore the broader struggle for black justice, equality, and freedom during the Revolutionary era.

In old Massachusetts, Salem Poor was born,
From the shackles of slavery, his spirit was torn.
Yet with grit and might, he broke the chains,
Became a hero, his legacy remains.

Purchasing freedom, he paved his own way,
A patriot soldier, he'd proudly display.
In Bunker Hill's battle, he stood firm and strong,
Fighting for freedom, where courage belongs.

Now if Salem Poor were still around,
In modern times, where dreams abound,
Perhaps he'd be a leader, wise and bold,
With stories of valor, proudly told.

In boardrooms or classrooms, he'd take his place,
Inspiring others with his grace.
A beacon of hope, a guiding light,
In a world where wrongs beg for right.

Today, we honor his brave stand,
And the courage he showed, so grand.
Let us emulate his spirit true,
And make our ancestors proud, too.

So, men of today, let's heed his call,
Stand tall, stand strong, and stand for all.
For in Salem Poor's legacy, we find,
The power to uplift all humankind.

Frederick Douglass (1818 – 1895) was a prominent African American social reformer, abolitionist, orator, writer, and statesman. Born into slavery in Maryland, he escaped to the North in 1838, where he became a leading voice in the abolitionist movement. Douglass's powerful oratory and incisive writings, including his first autobiography, "Narrative of the Life of Frederick Douglass, an American Slave" (1845), exposed the brutal realities of slavery and argued compellingly for its abolition. Douglass was a tireless advocate for black justice, equality, and freedom. He supported women's suffrage and held several public offices, including U.S. Marshal and Recorder of Deeds for the District of Columbia, and was appointed Minister Resident and Consul General to Haiti. He also published influential abolitionist newspapers such as "The North Star." Throughout his life, Douglass used his platform to fight against racial discrimination and for the full inclusion of African Americans in American society. His speeches and writings not only inspired many to join the abolitionist cause but also laid the groundwork for future civil rights movements. His enduring legacy is that of a champion for human rights and a pivotal figure in America's journey toward equality and justice for all.

In the annals of history, Frederick Douglass stands tall,
A beacon of justice, he answered the call.
With eloquent speeches and words that inspire,
He fueled the flames of freedom's fire.

An abolitionist hero, with courage untold,
He fought for the rights of the oppressed, bold.
Through trials and tribulations, he never backed down,
His legacy shines, a radiant crown.

If Douglass were here in our modern-day scene,
Perhaps he'd be on screens, sharp and keen.
A voice for the voiceless, in the halls of power,
Championing justice every hour.

Or maybe he'd write, with a pen in hand,
Crafting words of wisdom, across the land.
His voice still resonating, in every word he'd pen,
Guiding us forward, again and again.

So, men of today, let's take a cue,
From Douglass's courage, so tried and true.
Let's stand up for justice, with hearts aglow,
And make our ancestors proud, as we go.

Booker T. Washington (1856 – 1915) was a seminal African American educator, author, orator, and advisor to multiple U.S. presidents. Born into slavery in Virginia, Washington became one of the most influential black leaders of his time, particularly through his advocacy for vocational education as a means to achieve economic self-reliance and empowerment for African Americans. Washington's most notable achievement was the founding of the Tuskegee Normal and Industrial Institute (now Tuskegee University) in Alabama in 1881. Under his leadership, Tuskegee became a model for vocational education, emphasizing practical skills and self-help. He believed that economic progress, through industrial and agricultural education, was essential for African Americans to gain respect and improve their social status in post-Reconstruction America. His 1895 Atlanta Compromise speech advocated for black progress through education and entrepreneurship, rather than immediate social integration and political rights. This pragmatic approach garnered both support and criticism; some praised his emphasis on self-reliance, while others, like W.E.B. Du Bois, criticized him for not demanding immediate civil rights. In addition to his educational work, Washington was an advisor to Presidents Theodore Roosevelt and William Howard Taft, significantly influencing the administration's policies toward African Americans. He also authored several books, including his autobiography, "Up from Slavery" (1901), which detailed his philosophy and the challenges he overcame. Booker T. Washington's legacy lies in his relentless efforts to improve the economic and educational conditions of African Americans. He advocated for a strategic, long-term approach to achieving racial equality and justice.

In the halls of fame, Booker T. reigns,
A legacy of wisdom, hard work, and gains.
With a twinkle in his eye and a wit so sharp,
He carved his path through the darkest of arcs.

At Tuskegee's helm, he stood so tall,
Empowering minds, breaking down every wall.
"Education and self-reliance," he'd say,
Keys to unlock freedom's golden bay.

If Booker T. were here, oh, what a sight,
Guiding us through this modern plight.
In boardrooms and classrooms, his voice would ring,
Empowering all, regardless of skin.

He'd strut through the streets with a jaunty sway,
Teaching us all to seize the day.
"Black excellence!" he'd loudly proclaim,
In every endeavor, striving for acclaim.

So let's raise a toast to Booker T. bold,
His lessons timeless, never growing old.
For in his footsteps, we find our stride,
With education and grit as our guide.

To every man of today, here's the cue,

Emulate Booker T., make Black men proud too.

With determination and dreams held high,

We'll honor his legacy, reaching for the sky!

Thurgood Marshall (1908 – 1993) was a pioneering African American lawyer, civil rights activist, and the first African American Supreme Court Justice. Born in Baltimore, Maryland, Marshall graduated from Howard University School of Law in 1933, where he was mentored by Charles Hamilton Houston, a prominent civil rights lawyer. Marshall's most notable achievement was his role as the lead attorney for the NAACP in the landmark Supreme Court case Brown v. Board of Education (1954). His compelling arguments led to the Court's unanimous decision declaring racial segregation in public schools unconstitutional, a significant victory in the fight for civil rights and a major step towards desegregation. Throughout his career, Marshall argued and won numerous cases before the

Supreme Court, establishing legal precedents that advanced civil rights. These included Shelley v. Kraemer (1948), which struck down racially restrictive housing covenants, and Smith v. Allwright (1944), which ended the use of whites-only primaries in Texas. In 1967, President Lyndon B. Johnson appointed Marshall to the U.S. Supreme Court, where he served until 1991. As a Justice, Marshall continued to advocate for individual rights, equality, and social justice, often voicing strong support for affirmative action, women's rights, and the rights of criminal defendants. Thurgood Marshall's legacy is characterized by his unwavering commitment to justice, equality, and freedom for African Americans. His legal victories and tenure on the Supreme Court profoundly influenced the advancement of civil rights in the United States.

In the halls of justice, Thurgood's name resounds,
A titan of rights, breaking segregation's bounds.
With wit and wisdom, he fought the good fight,
For equality and justice, his beacon of light.

As the first black justice, his legacy shines bright,
In robes of honor, he stood for what's right.
But if Thurgood were here, what would he be?
Perhaps still fighting, with humor and glee.

In courtrooms or classrooms, his voice would resound,
Championing justice, on higher ground.
But maybe he'd kick back, with a smile so wide,
Cracking jokes and stories, with humble pride.

Today's men should heed his noble call,
Stand tall, stand proud, and break down each wall.
Embrace diversity, fight for what's fair,
In every action, show that you care.

So let's raise a toast, to Marshall's great name,
In history's pages, forever aflame.
A sweet tribute to a legend, so true,
Thurgood, we thank you, for all that you do!

Nat Turner

Nat Turner (1800 – 1831) was an enslaved African American who led a significant slave rebellion in Virginia in 1831. Born into slavery, Turner was deeply religious and believed he was chosen by God to lead his people out of bondage. On August 21, 1831, Turner and his followers initiated a rebellion in Southampton County, Virginia, which resulted in the deaths of approximately 60 white people. The uprising was suppressed within a few days, but Turner eluded capture until October 30, 1831. He was subsequently tried, convicted, and executed on November 11, 1831. Turner's rebellion had profound repercussions. It intensified the national debate over slavery and led to stricter slave laws and harsher enforcement of existing codes in the South, aiming to prevent any future insurrections. In the North, it fueled the abolitionist movement, bringing greater attention to the injustices of slavery and galvanizing efforts to end it. Though his methods were violent, Nat Turner is remembered for his resistance against the brutal system of slavery and his willingness to fight for freedom and justice. His legacy is complex, symbolizing both the desperate struggle for liberation and the extreme measures taken in the face of systemic oppression.

In memory of Nat Turner, let's spin a tale,
Of a man who dared to rise, to rebel, to prevail.
In eighteen thirty-one, he shook the chains of slavery's
yoke,
His courage echoed loud, it was no mere joke.

Nat Turner, bold and brave, in history's bright light,
Led a fierce rebellion, fought with all his might.
His actions spoke of justice, of freedom's sacred call,
In his heart, no chains could bind, no oppressor could
enthrall.

If Nat Turner walked among us now, what would he do?
Perhaps he'd lead with wisdom, inspire me and you.
He'd raise his voice for justice, against oppression's
cruel might,
His spirit would ignite the flames, for every human
right.

In every march for justice, in every cry for change,
Nat Turner's spirit dances, across the winds of range.
For men today, his legacy, a beacon burning bright,
To stand against injustice, to fight for what is right.

So let's honor Nat Turner, with laughter and with song,
For though he's gone, his legacy forever strong.
Let's emulate his courage, his spirit bold and true,
And make our black men proud, in everything we do.

Harriet Tubman (1822 – 1913) was an American abolitionist and political activist best known for her role in the Underground Railroad, a network of secret routes and safe houses used to help enslaved African Americans escape to free states and Canada. Born into slavery in Maryland, Tubman escaped to Philadelphia in 1849. Over a decade, Tubman made approximately 13 missions to rescue around 70 enslaved people, including family and friends, demonstrating extraordinary courage and resourcefulness. She became known as "Moses" for leading her people to freedom. During the Civil War, Tubman served as a scout, nurse, and spy for the Union Army. Notably, she led an armed expedition in the Combahee River Raid, which liberated more than 700 enslaved people in South Carolina, making her the first woman to lead a military operation in the United States. After the war, Tubman continued to fight for justice and equality. She was an active participant in the women's suffrage movement, advocating for women's right to vote alongside prominent suffragists like Susan B. Anthony. Harriet Tubman's legacy is one of unwavering commitment to freedom, justice, and equality. Her heroic efforts in rescuing enslaved people and her contributions to the Union war effort and women's rights have made her an enduring symbol of courage and resilience in the struggle for human rights.

In memory of Harriet Tubman, let's sing a song,
Of courage, wit, and a journey so long.
She led with her heart, as a conductor so bold,
Guiding souls to freedom, stories untold.

Through forests dense and rivers wide,
She steered the path, no fear to hide.
With a lantern bright and a spirit pure,
She whispered hope, a steadfast lure.

But now, in the realm beyond our sight,
What's Harriet up to in her flight?
Perhaps she's leading angelic choirs,
Or teaching stars to dance in celestial fires.

Or maybe she's still on a mission grand,
Inspiring hearts in a timeless land.
As a cosmic spy, she'd gather secrets rare,
From galaxies afar to worlds beyond compare.

In battles fought on ethereal plains,
She'd rally troops with celestial reins.
A warrior queen, she'd lead with grace,
In the cosmic dance of time and space.

Yet, in her legacy, we find our cue,
To carry forth what she dared to do.
For women today, in every stride,
Can echo her courage, with hearts open wide.

Let's honor her memory, let it resound,
By lifting each other, united and bound.
In her footsteps, let us proudly tread,
Embracing all, no soul left unread.

So, here's to Harriet, a beacon so bright,
Guiding us through the darkest night.
May her spirit live on, forever renowned,
In the hearts of women, forever unbound.

Sojourner Truth (1797 – 1883) was an African American abolitionist and women's rights activist renowned for her powerful oratory and unwavering commitment to social justice. Born into slavery in New York as Isabella Baumfree, she escaped with her infant daughter in 1826 and gained her freedom in 1827. In 1843, she changed her name to Sojourner Truth and began traveling and speaking out against slavery and advocating for women's rights. Her most famous speech, "Ain't I a Woman?", delivered at the Ohio Women's Rights Convention in 1851, highlighted the intersection of racial and gender discrimination and has become a cornerstone in both abolitionist and feminist movements. Truth was deeply involved in the abolitionist movement, working alongside prominent figures like

Frederick Douglass and William Lloyd Garrison. She also supported the Union during the Civil War, helping to recruit black troops and advocating for the provision of supplies and fair treatment for black soldiers. After the war, Truth continued her advocacy, focusing on improving the lives of freed slaves. She campaigned for land grants from the federal government, arguing that former slaves deserved their own land to ensure economic independence. Sojourner Truth's legacy lies in her relentless fight for black justice, equality, and freedom, as well as her pioneering role in the women's rights movement. Her life and work have inspired generations of activists and continue to resonate in the ongoing struggles for racial and gender equality.

In honor of Sojourner Truth, let's gather 'round,
With laughter and tales, let our voices resound.
A fierce advocate for rights so true,
With wit and wisdom, she broke through.

From the shackles of slavery to the halls of might,
She fought for justice, with all her might.
Her famous words, "Ain't I a Woman?"
Rang loud and clear, like a resounding drum.

But what would Sojourner do today,
If she were still with us, leading the way?
Perhaps she'd be on the front lines still,
Championing causes with iron will.

Maybe she'd be a social media star,
Spreading truth and wisdom near and far.
With tweets and posts, she'd ignite the flame,
Of equality and justice, in her name.

Or perhaps she'd be a podcast queen,
With interviews and stories, bold and keen.
Her voice echoing through the digital sphere,
Inspiring hearts, dispelling fear.

But whatever her role in this modern age,
Her legacy lives on, on history's stage.
For women today, her example shines bright,
In the fight for justice, in the quest for rights.

So let's raise our voices, let's stand tall,
In the footsteps of Sojourner, we heed the call.
To champion equality, to break down the wall,
And make black women proud, once and for all.

Ida B. Wells (1862 – 1931) was a prominent African American journalist, educator, and civil rights activist renowned for her courageous fight against lynching and her advocacy for black justice, equality, and freedom. Born into slavery in Holly Springs, Mississippi, Wells grew up during the Reconstruction era and pursued a career in teaching and journalism. In the 1890s, Wells launched a crusade against lynching after three of her friends were brutally murdered by a mob. Her investigative journalism exposed the horrors of lynching and its use as a tool of racial terror against African Americans. She published her findings in pamphlets such as "Southern Horrors: Lynch Law in All

Its Phases" (1892) and "The Red Record" (1895), garnering national and international attention. Wells co-founded several key civil rights organizations, including the National Association of Colored Women (NACW) in 1896 and the National Association for the Advancement of Colored People (NAACP) in 1909, though she later distanced herself from the NAACP due to ideological differences. She also helped found the Negro Fellowship League, which provided support and services to African American migrants in Chicago. In addition to her anti-lynching campaign, Wells was a strong advocate for women's suffrage and worked to ensure that black women had a voice in the suffrage movement. She famously integrated a suffrage parade in Washington, D.C., in 1913, defying instructions to march in a segregated section. Ida B. Wells' legacy is marked by her fearless activism and her profound impact on the struggle for civil rights and social justice. Her relentless efforts to expose and combat racial violence and her dedication to equality and freedom have left an enduring mark on American history.

In a time of shadows, she dared to shine,
Ida B. Wells, a legend so divine.
With pen in hand, she waged a righteous fight,
Unveiling truths hidden in the darkest night.

In the land of Dixie, where injustice reigned,
Her words like thunder, they could not be restrained.
Through ink-stained pages, her courage unfurled,
Exposing the ugliness of a prejudiced world.

With wit and wisdom, she pierced through the veil,
Unraveling tales of horror and travail.
Lynching's grim specter, she dared to confront,
Her voice a beacon, for justice to hunt.

Co-founder of The National Association for the
Advancement of Colored People (NAACP),
She stood tall and answered the call.
For suffrage and rights, she fought with grace,
Leaving a legacy no time can erase.

If Ida were here, what would she pursue?
Perhaps still fighting, for rights overdue.
In an era of hashtags, tweets, and likes,
She'd harness the power of digital spikes.

But let's imagine, just for a laugh,
Ida B. Wells on a modern-day staff.
A podcast host with a mic in her hand,
Dishing out truth in a way oh-so grand!

To women today, her spirit we hail,
With courage and grace, may we set sail.
Emulate her fire, her strength, her flair,
And make black women proud everywhere!

Mary Church Terrell (1863 – 1954) was a prominent African American educator, writer, and civil rights activist dedicated to fighting for black justice, equality, and freedom. Born to former slaves in Memphis, Tennessee, she was one of the first African American women to earn a college degree, graduating from Oberlin College in 1884. Terrell was a founding member and the first president of the National Association of Colored Women (NACW) in 1896. Under her leadership, the NACW campaigned against lynching, promoted education, and advocated for women's suffrage and social reforms. She also played a crucial role in the founding of the National Association for the

Advancement of Colored People (NAACP) in 1909 and was actively involved in the organization's efforts to combat racial discrimination. As a writer and speaker, Terrell addressed issues of race and gender discrimination, promoting the rights of African Americans and women. Her autobiography, "A Colored Woman in a White World" (1940), highlighted her personal experiences with racism and sexism and her lifelong fight for justice. Terrell was also a pioneer in the fight for desegregation. In 1950, she filed a lawsuit against the segregated restaurants in Washington, D.C., leading to a landmark court decision in 1953 that ruled segregation in public places in the capital unconstitutional. Mary Church Terrell's legacy is marked by her tireless advocacy for civil rights and her significant contributions to advancing racial and gender equality in the United States. Her work laid the groundwork for future civil rights movements and continues to inspire activists today.

In the annals of history, a beacon does gleam,
Mary Church Terrell, a star in the dream.
From Oberlin's halls, she emerged with a gleam,
To champion her people, to stoke freedom's beam.

With class and with poise, she took up the cause,
Empowering others, breaking down laws.
In the upper echelons, she made her stand,
For justice and rights, across the land.

Co-founder, she was of movements so grand,
The National Association of Colored Women (NACW)
and The National Association for the Advancement
of Colored People (NAACP) hand in hand.
With each stride she took, she paved the way,
For a brighter tomorrow, come what may.

If Mary were here, what would she pursue?
Perhaps still organizing, rallying the crew.
In a world of hashtags and social media flare,
Her voice would ring out, bold and rare.

But let's imagine, just for a jest,
Mary Church Terrell put to the test.
A social media maven, with hashtags galore,
Spreading her message, engaging with more!

To women today, her example we hail,
With courage and grace, let's set sail.
Emulate her spirit, her fervor, her might,
And make black women proud, in the day and the
night!

W.E.B. Du Bois (1868 – 1963) was a pioneering African American sociologist, historian, civil rights activist, and writer. Born in Massachusetts, Du Bois became the first African American to earn a doctorate from Harvard University in 1895. Du Bois was a co-founder of the National Association for the Advancement of Colored People (NAACP) in 1909 and served as its director of publicity and research. He was the editor of the NAACP's magazine, The Crisis, which became a leading voice in the struggle for civil rights, advocating for anti-lynching legislation, equal educational opportunities, and voting rights for African Americans. As a scholar, Du Bois conducted groundbreaking research on race and sociology, challenging prevailing notions of racial inferiority. His seminal work, "The Souls of Black Folk" (1903), explored the psychological and social effects of racism on African Americans and emphasized the importance of education and political activism in achieving equality. Du Bois was also a fierce critic of Booker T. Washington's accommodationist approach to civil rights, advocating instead for full political, social, and economic equality for African Americans. He believed in the power of the "Talented Tenth," an educated elite, to lead the black community to social progress. Throughout his life, Du Bois fought tirelessly for black justice, equality, and freedom through his scholarly work and his activism. He was a leading intellectual figure in the early civil rights movement, and his ideas continue to influence discussions on race and social justice today.

In the pages of history, a titan did stand,
W.E.B. Du Bois, with pen in hand.
Sociologist, historian, editor, too,
His legacy's vast, his impact, it grew.

With intellect and passion, he reached for the skies.
On the board, in research, he took his stand,
With The Crisis in hand, he shaped the land.
W.E.B. Du Bois, a legend in his own right.

A scholar, a thinker, with Harvard's Ph.D. in hand,
He dared to dream and to understand.
Through "The Souls of Black Folk," his voice did ring,
Challenging injustice with every word he'd bring.

Co-founder of The National Association for the
Advancement of Colored People (NAACP),
He stood tall and strong,
Against discrimination, he fought all along.

In the Niagara Movement, he laid the ground,
For a future where equality would resound.
He carved out a space,
Pioneering paths through the darkest of night.

But let's imagine, in this whimsical verse,
If Du Bois were here, what could be worse?
Would he be on Twitter, sharing his thoughts?
Or on TikTok, showing his dance moves, a lot?

Perhaps he'd be hosting podcasts, spreading insight,
Or on YouTube, sparking debates day and night.
In a world of social media, his voice would be loud,
Inspiring change, making us all proud.

So, to men of today, a lesson we must heed,
From Du Bois' legacy, we must take the lead.
With courage and wisdom, let's stand up tall,
And strive to make a difference, for one and for all.

Let's emulate his spirit, his fire, his grace,
And continue the journey, to make this world a better
place.
For Du Bois showed us, through his tireless fight,
That justice and equality are worth the fight.

Dorothy Height (1912 – 2010) was a prominent African American civil rights and women's rights activist known for her lifelong dedication to fighting for black justice, equality, and freedom. Born in Virginia, Height became involved in social activism at an early age, joining the National Council of Negro Women (NCNW) in 1937. As president of the NCNW from 1957 to 1997, Height worked tirelessly to advance the rights and opportunities of African American women. She focused on issues such as education, economic empowerment, and voting rights, advocating for policies and programs that would improve the lives of black women and their communities. Height was a key organizer of the 1963 March on Washington for Jobs and Freedom, where she was the only woman to share the platform with Dr. Martin Luther King Jr. She played a crucial role in the civil rights movement, working alongside leaders like King to push for racial equality and justice. In addition to her civil rights work, Height was a vocal advocate for women's rights and gender equality. She co-founded the National Women's Political Caucus in 1971 and worked to ensure that African American women's voices and concerns were heard in the women's rights movement. Throughout her life, Dorothy Height received numerous awards and honors for her activism, including the Presidential Medal of Freedom in 1994 and the Congressional Gold Medal in 2004. Her legacy is one of courage, resilience, and unwavering commitment to social justice, and her contributions continue to inspire generations of activists fighting for equality and freedom.

In memory of Dorothy Height, let's weave a tale,
Of a woman who dared, who refused to fail.
Born in Richmond, in nineteen twelve,
Her spirit so strong, her will to delve.

She faced discrimination, an unjust plight,
Yet, she rose above, shining so bright.
In the civil rights fight, she took her stand,
With passion and grace, across the land.

As president of the National Council of
Negro Women (NCNW), she led the way,
For four decades strong, come what may.
Desegregating YWCA, her historic stride,
Injustice she battled, with unwavering pride.

Alongside King Jr., she marched, she fought,
For justice and rights, in every thought.
In '63, the march, a moment profound,
Though not given voice, her impact unbound.

Today, if Dorothy were here by our side,
She'd advocate still, with a heart open wide.
Against injustice, inequality's chains,
She'd raise her voice, where justice reigns.

For women today, her legacy gleams,
A beacon of hope, in the midst of dreams.
To emulate her, to stand tall and proud,
To speak for justice, clear and loud.

Let's honor her spirit, her unwavering light,
And strive for a world, where all is right.
Dorothy Height, forever we'll sing,
Of the change she brought, on freedom's wing.

Martin Luther King Jr. (1929 – 1968) was a towering figure in the American civil rights movement, renowned for his leadership in the struggle for black justice, equality, and freedom. Born in Atlanta, Georgia, King became a Baptist minister and rose to prominence as a charismatic and impassioned advocate for nonviolent protest. King's leadership of the Montgomery Bus Boycott in 1955 marked the beginning of his national prominence. The boycott, sparked by Rosa Parks' refusal to give up her bus seat to a white passenger, lasted over a year and ultimately led to the desegregation of Montgomery's public transportation system. In 1957, King helped found the Southern Christian Leadership Conference (SCLC), an organization committed to nonviolent direct action to achieve civil rights reform. He became its president and led numerous campaigns, including the Birmingham Campaign in 1963, which highlighted the brutality of segregationist practices and led to the passage of the Civil Rights Act of 1964. King's most famous speech, "I Have a Dream," delivered during the March on Washington for Jobs and Freedom in 1963, articulated his vision of racial harmony and equality. The march drew hundreds of thousands of supporters and played a pivotal role in the passage of the Civil Rights Act. Throughout his life, King faced violent opposition and was arrested numerous times for his activism. However, he remained committed to nonviolent resistance, inspired by Mahatma Gandhi's teachings. His commitment to peaceful protest and his vision of a beloved community where all people are treated with dignity and respect continue to inspire activists around the world. Martin Luther King Jr.'s legacy is one of courage, compassion, and unwavering dedication to justice. His leadership and sacrifice transformed America and continue to shape movements for social change today.

In the heart of history's grand parade,
Stands Martin Luther King Jr., unswayed.
With eloquence, he preached equality's song,
In the face of injustice, he stood strong.

His voice, a beacon in the darkest night,
Guiding the oppressed toward the light.
Through boycotts, marches, and speeches bold,
He fought for a future where all hearts hold.

In the realm of civil rights, he was a king,
Martin Luther's praises we all love to sing.
With his wisdom so bright, his heart full of cheer,
He fought for justice, year after year.

Marching in Montgomery, he took a bold stand,
With peace in his heart and love for his land.
The buses they halted, segregation they fought,
With courage and grace, their message was taught.

Then to Washington, D.C., he did stride,
His words like a river, flowing far and wide.
"I Have a Dream," he proclaimed with such might,
A vision of equality, shining so bright.

With the Civil Rights Act, a victory won,
The battle for justice was far from done.
And the Voting Rights Act, a triumph so sweet,
For every voice to be heard, in every street.

Now if Martin, the Nobel Laureate, were here,
What would he say?
Perhaps he'd tweet for justice with might,
Or host Zoom rallies to spark the fight.

With memes and gifs, he'd make us see,
That change begins with you and me.
He'd call for unity, for love to prevail,
Injustice to combat, and hatred to quail.

So let's honor his memory with laughter and song,
And keep fighting for justice all day long.
For in every action, big or small,
We can carry on Dr. King's call.

Medgar Evers (1925 – 1963) was a courageous civil rights activist who dedicated his life to fighting for black justice, equality, and freedom. Born in Mississippi, Evers served in World War II before attending college and becoming involved in the civil rights movement. Evers became the first field secretary for the Mississippi chapter of the NAACP (National Association for the Advancement of Colored People) in 1954. In this role, he worked tirelessly to organize voter registration drives, desegregate schools, and challenge racial discrimination in various forms. Evers faced considerable danger and harassment due to his activism. He and his family received numerous threats, and their home was targeted with gunfire and Molotov cocktails. Despite the dangers, Evers remained steadfast in his commitment to the cause. One of Evers' most notable achievements was his efforts to investigate and publicize racial violence and injustice in Mississippi. He documented numerous cases of police brutality, economic discrimination, and voter suppression, bringing national attention to the plight of African Americans in the segregated South. Tragically, Medgar Evers was assassinated outside his home in Jackson, Mississippi, on June 12, 1963, by a white supremacist named Byron De La Beckwith. His death sparked outrage and galvanized the civil rights movement, leading to increased activism and calls for justice. Although Evers did not live to see the full fruits of his labor, his legacy lives on as a symbol of courage, sacrifice, and determination in the struggle for racial equality. His death became a rallying cry for the civil rights movement and inspired generations of activists to continue the fight for justice and freedom.

In the heart of Mississippi, where the sun beats down,
Stood a man of courage, with a fearless crown.
Medgar Evers, his name echoes through time,
A champion for justice, in his prime.

With The National Association for the
Advancement of Colored People's (NAACP)
banner, he marched ahead,
Through the storm of bigotry, he firmly tread.

Voter drives, boycotts, his weapons of choice,
To fight segregation with a resounding voice.
Denied at first, Mississippi's gate,
But undeterred, he didn't hesitate.
But tragically taken, in a moment so dire,
His legacy lives on, brighter than fire.
If Medgar were here, what might he be?
Still fighting for justice, with laughter and glee.

Today's men can learn, from his noble stand,
To uphold dignity, across the land.
Embrace diversity, break down each wall,
In Medgar Evers' footsteps, stand tall.

So let's honor his memory, his spirit so true,
A sweet ode to Medgar, whom we hold dear.
Though he's gone, his legacy's bright,
Guiding us forward, towards what's right.

Malcolm X

Malcolm X (1925 – 1965) was a prominent African American activist and Muslim minister who played a significant role in the struggle for black justice, equality, and freedom. Born Malcolm Little in Nebraska, he rose to prominence as a leading figure in the Nation of Islam (NOI), a black nationalist religious organization, during the 1950s and early 1960s. Malcolm X's advocacy for black empowerment and self-defense made him a polarizing figure. He famously articulated the ideology of black nationalism, promoting the idea of black pride, self-determination, and the rejection of white supremacy. His speeches and writings, including his autobiography "The Autobiography of Malcolm X" (1965), became influential in shaping the consciousness of African Americans and challenging racial injustice. Malcolm X's break with the Nation of Islam in 1964 marked a significant turning point in his life and activism. He converted to Sunni Islam and adopted a more inclusive approach to civil rights, advocating for cooperation between all races in the struggle for equality. He founded the Organization of Afro-American Unity (OAAU), which sought to promote unity among African Americans and fight for human rights on a global scale. Tragically, Malcolm X was assassinated on February 21, 1965, while delivering a speech in New York City. His death robbed the world of one of its most dynamic and influential voices for black liberation. Malcolm X's legacy continues to inspire generations of activists and leaders in the fight against racial oppression and inequality. His unapologetic advocacy for black empowerment and his commitment to the pursuit of justice have left an indelible mark on the struggle for freedom and equality.

In the annals of history, a lion roared loud,
Malcolm X, with fire, his voice did astound.
Human rights activist, with a vision so clear,
Advocating for Black power, without any fear.

His speeches were thunder, his words like a storm,
Urging Black self-determination, a new norm.
With passion and fervor, he fought the good fight,
Empowering his people to stand up and unite.

In the heart of the struggle, he took his stand,
Championing Black pride across the land.
With words like thunder, he stirred the crowd,
Calling for justice, clear and loud.

Black nationalism beat within his chest,
As he fought for freedom, never to rest.
Self-reliance, his mantra, his creed,
Inspiring others to follow his lead.

But humor danced within his eyes,
A twinkle of mischief, a clever disguise.
For even in the midst of the fight,
He found joy in laughter, shining bright.

Imagine if Malcolm walked among us today,
Leading the charge in his own unique way.
Perhaps he'd be a voice for unity,
A bridge between cultures, a symbol of diversity.

Men of today, take heed and learn,
From Malcolm's legacy, let it burn.
Embrace your roots, stand tall and proud,
In every stride, let his spirit be loud.

For in his footsteps, we find our path,
A journey of courage, free from wrath.
So let us honor him, with deeds profound,
And make our ancestors proud, the world around.

Barack Obama (born August 4, 1961) is an American politician and attorney who served as the 44th President of the United States from 2009 to 2017. His election marked a historic moment as he became the first African American to hold the nation's highest office. Throughout his presidency, Obama pursued policies aimed at advancing racial justice, equality, and freedom. Some of his key achievements include:

1. Affordable Care Act (ACA): Obama signed the ACA, also known as Obamacare, into law in 2010. This landmark legislation aimed to expand access to healthcare coverage, including for millions of previously uninsured

Americans, many of whom were from marginalized communities.

2. Criminal Justice Reform: Obama took steps to address systemic issues within the criminal justice system, including signing the Fair Sentencing Act in 2010, which aimed to reduce disparities in sentencing for offenses involving crack cocaine versus powder cocaine.

3. Economic Recovery: In response to the Great Recession, Obama signed the American Recovery and Reinvestment Act in 2009, which aimed to stimulate economic growth, create jobs, and provide assistance to those most affected by the economic downturn, including minority communities.

4. Civil Rights and LGBTQ+ Rights: Obama supported and advocated for LGBTQ+ rights, including the repeal of the "Don't Ask, Don't Tell" policy, which prohibited openly gay individuals from serving in the military. He also publicly endorsed same-sex marriage, marking a significant milestone in the fight for LGBTQ+ equality.

5. Voting Rights: Obama spoke out against voter suppression efforts and supported measures to expand access to voting, including advocating for the restoration of the Voting Rights Act of

1965 following a Supreme Court decision that weakened its enforcement.

While Obama's presidency faced challenges and criticism, particularly from political opponents, his leadership represented a significant moment in American history. As the first African American president, Obama's election and tenure in office inspired hope and symbolized progress toward a more inclusive and equitable society.

In a land where dreams take flight,
Stood a man with hope so bright.
Barack Obama, his name we sing,
The 44th President, what a wonderful thing!

Born in Hawaii, with a smile so wide,
A diverse upbringing, a global ride.
From Occidental to Harvard Law School,
His journey was cool, never the fool.

In Illinois, he took a stand,
In the Senate, he lent a hand.
Then to the White House, he made his way,
History was made on that fateful day.

Affordable Care Act, a beacon of light,
Bin Laden's demise, justice took flight.
Same-sex marriage, a step forward we see,
Obama's legacy, a mark in history.

Now today, what does he do?
Continues to inspire others, like me and you.
Through his foundation, his voice still strong,
Injustice defeated, hope lives on.

So let's take a cue from this man so proud,
Let's stand tall, let's say it loud.
Black men, be proud, emulate his grace,
In every stride, in every race.

For Obama showed us what can be done,
With courage and love, we've already won.
So, here's to you, Barack, our guiding star,
In our hearts, you'll always lead us.

Kamala Harris (born October 20, 1964) is an American politician and attorney who has made significant contributions to the fight for justice, equality, and freedom, particularly for marginalized communities, including African Americans. Harris has achieved several milestones throughout her career:

1. Legal Career: Before entering politics, Harris served as a prosecutor in the Alameda County District Attorney's Office and later as the District Attorney of San Francisco. She became the first woman, first African American woman, and first South Asian American

woman to hold the position of California Attorney General in 2011.

2. Criminal Justice Reform: As Attorney General of California, Harris implemented various initiatives aimed at addressing systemic issues within the criminal justice system. She prioritized the reduction of recidivism rates, advocated for policies to address implicit bias, and worked to increase transparency and accountability in law enforcement.

3. U.S. Senate: In 2017, Harris was sworn in as a United States Senator from California, becoming the second African American woman and the first South Asian American woman to serve in the U.S. Senate. During her tenure, she championed numerous legislative efforts to advance civil rights, including co-sponsoring the George Floyd Justice in Policing Act and the Voting Rights Advancement Act.

4. Vice Presidency: In 2021, Kamala Harris made history as the first woman, first African American woman, and first Asian American woman to serve as Vice President of the United States under President Joe Biden. Her election to this position represented a significant breakthrough in American politics and

inspired hope for greater representation and diversity in leadership roles.

Throughout her career, Kamala Harris has been a vocal advocate for social justice, equality, and civil rights. While her record has faced scrutiny and criticism from some quarters, particularly regarding her prosecutorial history, her historic achievements and commitment to advancing justice for all Americans have cemented her legacy as a trailblazer in American politics.

In honor of Kamala Devi Harris, our guiding light,
A woman of strength, a beacon shining bright.
From Oakland's streets to the White House halls,
She answered the nation's hopeful calls.

An attorney, a senator, a leader with grace,
She carved her path with a determined pace.
Breaking barriers, shattering ceilings high,
With each stride, reaching for the sky.

As the 49th Vice President, history she made,
Her legacy forever in our hearts engraved.
First female, first Black, and Asian too,
Her achievements spark inspiration anew.

From healthcare to taxes, from laws to reform,
Her dedication never failed to perform.
In her footsteps, women proudly tread,
Following the path, she boldly led.

As we continue to fight for justice in America,
What would she do?
Perhaps champion women's reproductive rights.
Guiding with wisdom, speaking with power.

So, let's raise our voices, let's emulate her cause,
In her grace and steadfastness, we'll never be the same.
For Kamala showed us what women can do,
Making us proud, making history true.

Claudette Colvin (born September 5, 1939) is an African American woman who played a pivotal role in the civil rights movement, particularly in the fight against segregation and for black justice, equality, and freedom. On March 2, 1955, at the age of 15, Claudette Colvin refused to give up her seat on a segregated bus in Montgomery, Alabama, nine months before Rosa Parks' similar act of defiance. Colvin was arrested and charged with violating segregation laws, sparking outrage and drawing attention to the injustice of racial segregation on public transportation. Colvin's courageous act of resistance inspired and galvanized the African American community in Montgomery. Her case, along with Rosa Parks, led to the Montgomery Bus Boycott, a year-long protest against segregation on buses that ultimately resulted in the desegregation of the city's public transportation system. Although Colvin's role in the Montgomery Bus Boycott was overshadowed by Rosa Parks, her bravery and activism laid the groundwork for the civil rights movement and demonstrated the power of individual resistance against injustice. Claudette Colvin's contributions to the civil rights movement remind us of the courage and determination of ordinary people who fought for equality and justice in the face of adversity. Her legacy continues to inspire activists and advocates for social change today.

In Montgomery town, where history's spun,
Lies a tale of courage, of battles won.
Before Rosa's name filled the fame's cup,
There was Claudette Colvin, standing up.

A teenager bold, with a fiery spark,
Refused to yield on that bus embark.
To a white passenger, she'd not give way,
Injustice challenged, come what may!

Now imagine Claudette, if she were active,
In today's world, oh, what would appear?
Perhaps leading rallies, with passion ablaze,
Guiding the fight through these modern days.

Would she tweet her thoughts, in bold defiance,
Or organize marches with peaceful alliance?
Maybe on screens, she'd voice her stance,
Urging for justice with every chance.

Black women of today, take heed,
Claudette's legacy is one we need.
Emulate her courage, her strength untold,
Stand tall, speak up, let your voices unfold.

In every stride, in every act,
Keep her spirit alive, that's a fact.
For Claudette Colvin paved the way,
For a brighter tomorrow, come what may!

Rosa Parks (1913 – 2005) was a prominent civil rights activist known for her pivotal role in the Montgomery Bus Boycott, a significant event in the fight against segregation and for black justice, equality, and freedom. On December 1, 1955, Parks refused to give up her seat to a white passenger on a segregated bus in Montgomery, Alabama, as was required by Jim Crow laws. Her courageous act of defiance led to her arrest and sparked outrage within the African American community. The Montgomery Bus Boycott, organized in response to Parks' arrest, lasted for 381 days and was a key moment in the civil rights movement. Led by figures like Martin Luther King Jr., the boycott aimed to challenge racial segregation on public transportation and drew national attention to the injustice of segregation laws. Parks' actions and the success of the Montgomery Bus Boycott ultimately led to a Supreme Court ruling in 1956 that declared segregation on public buses unconstitutional, marking a significant victory in the fight against racial discrimination. Rosa Parks' bravery and determination to stand up against injustice made her an iconic figure in the civil rights movement. Her role in the Montgomery Bus Boycott and her lifelong commitment to activism continue to inspire generations of individuals fighting for equality and justice.

In Tuskegee, Alabama, on a February morn,
A hero was born, destined to adorn
The pages of history with courage profound,
Rosa Parks, with a spirit resolute and unbound.

In '55, on a Montgomery bus's seat,
She took a stand, with unwavering feat.
Refusing to yield, to injustice and hate,
Her defiance ignited a mighty debate.

With Dr. King and the Montgomery
Improvement Association (MIA) by her side,
She sparked a movement, a nationwide tide.
The Montgomery Bus Boycott, a rallying cry,
For equality and justice, reaching the sky.

Beyond those bus seats, her voice did resound,
In The National Association for the Advancement of
Colored People's (NAACP) halls, her activism found.
Challenging laws, with her brave legal fight,
She showed the world that wrongs can be made right.

Now, if Rosa were here, what would she do?
I imagine she'd fight for equality anew.
In a world still divided, she'd lend her voice,
To empower the oppressed, to make a choice.

She'd stand with the women, of every shade,
Encouraging them, not to be afraid.
To speak up, to rise, and to take their place,
In shaping a future, filled with grace.

So let us remember, her legacy grand,
And strive to emulate, her courageous stand.
For women today, of every hue,
Can make Rosa proud, by being true.

John Lewis (1940 – 2020) was a towering figure in the American civil rights movement and a lifelong advocate for black justice, equality, and freedom. Born in Alabama, Lewis became involved in activism at a young age, inspired by the teachings of Martin Luther King Jr. and the nonviolent principles of the movement. As a leader of the Student Nonviolent Coordinating Committee (SNCC), Lewis played a key role in organizing and participating in numerous protests and demonstrations, including the Freedom Rides and the March on Washington in 1963. He was the youngest speaker at the March on Washington, where he delivered his iconic speech calling for racial justice and equality. One of Lewis's most notable achievements came on March 7, 1965, when he led over 600 peaceful protesters in a march for voting rights from Selma to Montgomery, Alabama. The march, known as "Bloody Sunday," was met with brutal violence from law enforcement, including Lewis being severely beaten, but it sparked national outrage and led to the passage of the Voting Rights Act of 1965. Lewis's commitment to civil rights and social justice continued throughout his life. He served as a U.S. Representative for Georgia's 5th congressional district from 1987 until his death in 2020, becoming known as the "conscience of the Congress." In Congress, he advocated for voting rights, healthcare reform, and gun control, among other issues, and continued to fight against racial discrimination and inequality. John Lewis's legacy is one of courage, resilience, and unwavering dedication to justice. His lifelong commitment to nonviolent protest and his tireless efforts to advance civil rights have left an indelible mark on American history and continue to inspire activists around the world.

In the tapestry of history, a hero we find,
John Lewis, with courage, gentle, and kind.
A leader of marches, a voice for the free,
His legacy sahines for all to see.

From the halls of Student Nonviolent
Coordinating Committee (SNCC) to the marches so
grand,
He led with courage, a true guiding hand.
On "Bloody Sunday," on that bridge, he did stand,
A warrior for justice in a troubled land.

With each step on the road from Selma to Montgomery,
He fought for rights, never wavering nor wary.
His spirit indomitable, his cause ever clear,
For equality and justice, he held dear.

But in humor's embrace, let's envision a scene,
Where John Lewis now reigns, still noble and keen.
Perhaps he'd debate with Lincoln on rights profound,
Or teach MLK some dance moves, so renowned.

In Congress, perhaps, he'd be raising his voice,
For voting rights, justice, and the people's choice.
A mentor to many, a beacon so bright,
Guiding the way with his wisdom and light.

And to men of today, a lesson to learn,
From Lewis's legacy, let it brightly burn.
To stand up for justice, to speak out with pride,
And make black men proud, with each step we stride.

So, let's raise our voices, in honor we sing,
Of John Lewis, whose legacy forever will ring.
Sweet and funny, his spirit shall endure,
A champion for justice, forevermore.

Coretta Scott King (1927 – 2006) was an influential civil rights leader, activist, and author who made significant contributions to the fight for black justice, equality, and freedom, both alongside her husband, Martin Luther King Jr., and as a leader in her own right. As the wife of Martin Luther King Jr., Coretta Scott King played a vital role in the civil rights movement. She supported her husband and participated in marches, demonstrations, and other activities aimed at challenging racial discrimination and segregation. After her husband's assassination in 1968, she continued his work, becoming a prominent advocate for racial and economic justice, peace, and nonviolence. Coretta Scott King co-founded and served as the first president of the Martin Luther King Jr. Center for Nonviolent Social Change, established in 1968 to promote her husband's legacy and advance his philosophy of nonviolent resistance. Under her leadership, the center became a hub for civil rights education, activism, and community engagement. In addition to her activism, Coretta Scott King was a passionate advocate for women's rights, LGBTQ+ rights, and economic justice. She spoke out against poverty, war, and discrimination in all its forms, emphasizing the interconnectedness of various struggles for justice and equality. Coretta Scott King's dedication to social justice and her tireless efforts to build a more equitable and inclusive society have left an enduring legacy. Her leadership and advocacy continue to inspire activists around the world in the ongoing fight for human rights and equality.

In honor of Coretta Scott King, a radiant light,
Whose courage and grace shone ever so bright.
The wife of Martin, yet a queen in her own right,
She carried on his legacy with all her might.

In her heart, the flame of justice burned true,
She fought for rights, for peace, for me and you.
Through trials and triumphs, she never withdrew,
Her voice, a beacon, for justice to pursue.

If Coretta were here, what would she do?
Perhaps lead rallies or write a book or two.
Championing causes, breaking barriers anew,
Her spirit alive in all that we pursue.

To women today, her legacy calls,
In every struggle, in every halls.
Let's carry her torch, let our voices be bold,
In the fight for justice, let our stories be told.

Black women, rise up, let your voices resound,
In every endeavor, let your brilliance be found.
Coretta's legacy, let it forever be renowned,
In every victory, in every battleground.

So here's to Coretta, forever our guide,
In her footsteps, let us bravely stride.
With love and laughter, let our spirits be tied,
In her memory, let justice be our pride.

Angela Davis (born January 26, 1944) is an influential scholar, activist, and author known for her lifelong commitment to fighting for black justice, equality, and freedom. Davis emerged as a prominent figure in the civil rights movement of the 1960s and 1970s and remains a leading voice in contemporary struggles against racism, sexism, and other forms of oppression. Davis's activism spans decades and encompasses a wide range of social justice issues. As a member of the Communist Party USA and the Black Panther Party, she advocated for the rights of African Americans, particularly those impacted by police brutality and systemic racism. She also worked tirelessly to address issues such as prison reform, economic inequality, and gender discrimination. One of Davis's most notable achievements came in 1972 when she was acquitted of charges related to a prison escape and kidnapping case. Her trial garnered international attention and became a symbol of resistance against state repression and injustice. Following her acquittal, Davis continued her activism and scholarship, using her platform to amplify the voices of marginalized communities and advocate for radical social change. Throughout her career, Davis has written extensively on topics such as race, feminism, and abolition. Her books, including "Women, Race, & Class" and "Are Prisons Obsolete?, " have had a profound impact on academia and activism, challenging dominant narratives and inspiring generations of scholars and activists. Angela Davis's legacy is characterized by her unwavering commitment to justice and liberation for all oppressed people. Her fearless advocacy, scholarship, and activism continue to inspire individuals and movements around the world in the ongoing struggle for equality and freedom.

In the realm of justice, bold and free,
Stands Angela Davis, with a fierce decree.
Activist, scholar, a spirit unbound,
In the fight for justice, she's renowned.

With wisdom and wit, she took her stand,
Against oppression, with a mighty hand.
Her voice, a beacon, in the darkest night,
Guiding us all toward what's just and right.

If Angela were still active, what mischief and glee,
Would she stir up in the name of equity?
Perhaps she'd teach, with passion ablaze,
Or lead marches in her own sassy ways.

In the halls of academia, she'd surely roam,
Challenging norms, making waves in her home.
With books and lectures, she'd spread her creed,
Empowering all to fight for what they need.

To women of today, her message rings clear,
Embrace your power, let your voices cheer.
In every struggle, in every fight,
Stand up for justice with all your might.

Black women, rise up, let your brilliance shine,
In every moment, let your spirit align.
With Angela's spirit, let us be endowed,
In her footsteps, let us make her proud.

So here's to Angela, with love and jest,
In her honor, let's give it our best.
With laughter and joy, let's carry her torch,
In the fight for justice, let's never retort.

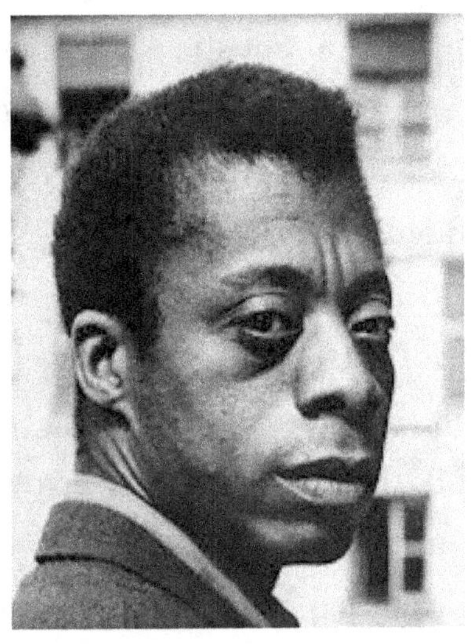

James Baldwin (1924 – 1987) was a prolific African American writer, playwright, and activist who, through his literary works and social commentary, made significant contributions to the fight for black justice, equality, and freedom. Baldwin's writing explored themes of race, sexuality, and identity in America, shedding light on the complexities of the black experience and challenging societal norms and prejudices. His novels, essays, and plays, including "Go Tell It on the Mountain" (1953), "Notes of a Native Son" (1955), and "The Fire Next Time" (1963), are considered seminal works in American literature and have had a profound impact on readers and scholars alike. One of Baldwin's most notable achievements was his role as a leading voice in the civil rights movement of the 1950s and 1960s. He used his platform as a writer and public intellectual to speak out against racial injustice and advocate for social change, often addressing issues such as police brutality, segregation, and the struggle for civil rights. Baldwin's activism extended beyond the United States. He also spoke out against colonialism and apartheid in Africa and South Africa, respectively. He traveled extensively and engaged in dialogue with other activists and intellectuals around the world, working to build bridges across racial and cultural divides. James Baldwin's legacy is characterized by his fearless commitment to truth-telling and his unwavering dedication to the fight for justice and equality. His works continue to resonate with readers today, inspiring new generations of activists and scholars in the ongoing struggle for freedom and liberation.

In the realm of words, where truth resides,
Lives James Baldwin, with his powerful strides.
A writer, a critic, with a fiery pen,
His legacy lives on, inspiring men.

From Harlem's streets to the world's stage,
Baldwin's voice echoed with wisdom and rage.
Exploring race, sexuality, identity's dance,
His words still ignite, they still entrance.

If James were here, what tales would he spin?
Perhaps tackling issues with a sly grin.
In today's world, his voice would resound,
With insight and humor, profound.

He'd challenge norms, provoke thought,
Injustice and bigotry, he'd always fought.
With essays and novels, he'd stir the pot,
Calling out society's every fraught.

To men of today, his message is clear,
Embrace your truth, let your voices steer.
In every struggle, in every stand,
Be brave like Baldwin, make your demands.

Black men, rise up, let your brilliance gleam,
In every endeavor, let your spirit stream.
With Baldwin's spirit, let us be endowed,
In his footsteps, let's make him proud.

So here's to James, with laughter and cheer,
His words still echo, they still endear.
With humor and insight, let's carry his flame,
In the fight for justice, let's never be tame.

Audre Lorde (1934 – 1992) was a trailblazing African American writer, poet, and activist known for her pioneering work in advocating for black justice, equality, and freedom, particularly within the context of intersectional feminism and LGBTQ+ rights. Lorde's poetry and prose explored themes of race, gender, sexuality, and identity, providing a powerful voice for marginalized communities. Her writings, including collections such as "The Black Unicorn" (1978) and "Sister Outsider" (1984), challenged prevailing societal norms and shed light on the experiences of black women and other oppressed groups. As a prominent activist, Lorde played a crucial role in advancing civil rights, feminism, and LGBTQ+ rights. She co-founded the Kitchen Table: Women of Color Press, a publishing collective dedicated to amplifying the voices of women of color, and was active in organizations such as the National Coalition of Black Lesbians and Gays. One of Lorde's most notable achievements was her advocacy for intersectionality, the idea that social identities intersect and interact to shape individuals' experiences of oppression and privilege. She emphasized the importance of recognizing and addressing multiple forms of discrimination, including racism, sexism, homophobia, and classism, in the fight for justice and equality. Lorde's legacy is marked by her courage, resilience, and unwavering commitment to social justice. Her writings and activism continue to inspire activists and scholars in the ongoing struggle for liberation and equality for all.

In the realm of verse, where magic's unfurled,
Audre Lorde's poetry, a precious world.
With words like spells, she wove her tale,
Challenging norms, she dared to prevail.

A poet, an essayist, with insight divine,
Her works like stars in a darkened sky shine.
Race, gender, and sexuality's plight,
In her words, they found their rightful height.

If Audre were here, oh, what would she do?
Perhaps write verses to make us all coo.
Or pen essays that pierce through the noise,
With humor and wisdom, her unique voice.

In today's world, her presence would soar,
Inspiring others to fight for much more.
With pen in hand, she'd lead the charge,
For equality, justice, she'd urge.

To women today, her message is clear,
Embrace your power, let your voices steer.
In every battle, in every quest,
Be bold like Lorde, stand with your chest.

Black women, rise up, let your brilliance shine,
In every moment, let your spirit align.
With Audre's spirit, let's make our stand,
In her footsteps, let's paint the land.

So here's to Audre, with laughter and cheer,
Her legacy lives on, year after year.
With humor and grace, let's carry her flame,
In the fight for justice, let's stake our claim.

Bayard Rustin (1912 – 1987) was a key figure in the American civil rights movement and a leading advocate for black justice, equality, and freedom. Rustin's contributions were wide-ranging and impactful, though his role was often overlooked or marginalized due to his identity as an openly gay man in an era when LGBTQ+ rights were not widely recognized. One of Rustin's most significant achievements was his role as the chief organizer of the 1963 March on Washington for Jobs and Freedom, where Dr. Martin Luther King Jr. delivered his iconic "I Have a Dream" speech. Rustin played a crucial behind-the-scenes role in coordinating logistics, mobilizing participants, and ensuring the march's success. Rustin was also a proponent of nonviolent protest and civil disobedience, drawing inspiration from his study of Mahatma Gandhi's philosophy of nonviolence. He worked closely with Dr. King as an advisor and strategist, advocating for nonviolent direct action as a powerful tool for social change. Throughout his life, Rustin fought against racial discrimination and segregation, participating in numerous campaigns and demonstrations for civil rights. He also worked to advance LGBTQ+ rights, co-founding organizations such as the Mattachine Society and advocating for the decriminalization of homosexuality. Despite facing discrimination and persecution due to his sexual orientation, Rustin remained steadfast in his commitment to justice and equality. His legacy is one of courage, resilience, and unwavering dedication to the fight for black liberation and LGBTQ+ rights, and his contributions continue to inspire activists and advocates for social change today.

In memoriam of Bayard Rustin, we sing,
A man whose legacy makes our hearts ring.
With a twinkle in his eye and courage so bold,
He orchestrated change, breaking barriers of old.

In '63, he led the charge, oh so grand,
Marching on Washington, hand in hand.
His strategy and wit, a beacon so bright,
Guiding the movement toward justice's light.

With nonviolent resistance, he paved the way,
Fighting for rights, come what may.
An openly gay leader, he stood tall and true,
Teaching us all, there's power in being you.

Now, if Bayard were here, what would he do?
Perhaps organize rallies, stirring hearts anew.
Advocating for justice, with passion and flair,
His voice ringing out, cutting through despair.

But let's not forget, his lessons endure,
In today's struggles, his wisdom pure.
Men of today, take heed and learn,
From Bayard's example, let your courage burn.

Emulate his spirit, his strength, his grace,
And make Black men proud, in every place.
For in honoring his legacy, we carry the flame,
Bayard Rustin's legacy, forever aflame.

Fannie Lou Hamer (1917 – 1977) was a courageous civil rights leader and voting rights activist who made significant contributions to the fight for black justice, equality, and freedom, particularly in Mississippi during the 1960s. Hamer's activism began when she became involved with the Student Nonviolent Coordinating Committee (SNCC) in the early 1960s. She became known for her powerful oratory and unwavering commitment to securing voting rights for African Americans in the segregated South. One of Hamer's most notable achievements was her role in organizing the Mississippi Freedom Summer in 1964, a campaign to register black voters in the state. Despite facing threats, intimidation, and violence, Hamer and other activists courageously worked to challenge barriers to voting and empower African Americans to exercise their constitutional rights. Hamer's activism led to her being arrested and beaten multiple times, including during her famous testimony at the 1964 Democratic National Convention, where she described the brutal violence she and other activists endured while attempting to register to vote. In addition to her work on voting rights, Hamer was also a vocal advocate for economic justice and education. She helped establish the Mississippi Freedom Democratic Party (MFDP), which challenged the all-white Democratic Party delegation from Mississippi and fought for racial representation within the party. Fannie Lou Hamer's legacy is one of courage, resilience, and unwavering dedication to justice. Her tireless efforts to expand voting rights and empower African Americans have left an indelible mark on American history and continue to inspire activists and advocates for civil rights and social justice today.

In memory of Fannie Lou Hamer, we celebrate,
A woman of strength, who wouldn't hesitate.
From sharecropper's fields to the DNC stage,
Her voice rang out, ignited the rage.

In '64, she stood tall and bold,
Speaking truth to power, breaking the mold.
Co-founder of the Mississippi Freedom
Democratic Party (MFDP), daring and new,
Fighting for rights, for me and for you.

With fiery passion, she fought the fight,
For Black voting rights, with all her might.
Her testimony shook the nation's core,
Opening eyes, demanding more.

Now, if Fannie were here, what would she do?
Marching for justice, leading the crew.
Rallying women, with a powerful voice,
Championing rights, making a choice.

But let's not forget, her legacy lives on,
In every woman, rising at dawn.
Embrace her spirit, her courage, her flame,
And make Black women proud, in every game.

For in honoring her, we honor us all,
Fannie Lou Hamer, standing tall.

Septima Poinsette Clark (1898 – 1987) was a pioneering educator and civil rights activist who made significant contributions to the fight for black justice, equality, and freedom, particularly through her work in education and voter registration. Clark's activism began in the early 20th century when she became a teacher in the segregated schools of South Carolina. Despite facing discrimination and limitations on her ability to teach, Clark remained dedicated to providing quality education to African American students. One of Clark's most notable achievements was her work with the Highlander Folk School, an adult education center in Tennessee that focused on social justice issues. As the director of Highlander's Citizenship School program, Clark played a key role in training thousands of African

Americans to pass literacy tests and register to vote, empowering them to participate in the democratic process and challenge segregation laws. Clark's innovative approach to education, which combined literacy training with lessons on civil rights and political empowerment, became a model for grassroots organizing and community activism. Her work laid the groundwork for the civil rights movement and helped pave the way for the Voting Rights Act of 1965, which removed barriers to voting for African Americans in the South. In addition to her activism, Clark was a founding member of the Southern Christian Leadership Conference (SCLC) and worked closely with leaders like Dr. Martin Luther King Jr. to advance the cause of civil rights. She continued to advocate for educational equity and social justice throughout her life, leaving a lasting legacy of empowerment through education. Septima Poinsette Clark's contributions to the civil rights movement are a testament to her courage, resilience, and unwavering commitment to justice. Her pioneering work in education and voter registration continues to inspire activists and educators in the ongoing struggle for equality and freedom.

In honor of Septima Clark, let's raise a cheer,
A beacon of wisdom, oh so clear.
With books in one hand and justice in mind,
She paved the way for the oppressed to find.

An educator at heart, she taught with grace,
Empowering minds, whatever the place.
Citizenship schools, her ingenious plan,
Empowering voters, woman, and man.

In the fight for rights, she never backed down,
Mentoring Rosa Parks, a legend renowned.
With kindness and wit, she led the way,
Shaping tomorrow, come what may.

If Septima were here, what would she do?
Harnessing knowledge, breaking barriers too.
Advocating for change, with passion aflame,
Inspiring women to stake their claim.

So let's heed her call, her legacy bright,
Empower others, with all our might.
In every action, let justice resound,
Septima's spirit, forever unbound.

For in honoring her, we honor our creed,
Septima Poinsette Clark, a champion indeed.

Mary McLeod Bethune (1875 – 1955) was a pioneering educator, civil rights leader, and political activist who dedicated her life to fighting for black justice, equality, and freedom. Bethune was born to formerly enslaved parents in South Carolina and faced significant challenges growing up in poverty. Despite these obstacles, she pursued an education and became one of the first African American women to attend college. In 1904, she founded the Daytona Normal and Industrial Institute for Negro Girls in Florida, which later merged with the Cookman Institute to become Bethune-Cookman College. This institution provided African American students with access to quality education and voca-tional training. One of Bethune's most notable achievements was her role as a leader in the National Association of Colored Women (NACW), where she advocated for women's suffrage, racial equality, and social reform. She also served as the president of the National Council of Negro Women (NCNW), an organization she founded in 1935 to address issues affecting African American women and families. Bethune's activism extended to politics, and she was a trusted advisor to several U.S. presidents, including Franklin D. Roosevelt. In 1936, she became the highest-ranking African American woman in the federal government when she was appointed as director of the Division of Negro Affairs of the National Youth Administration. Throughout her life, Mary McLeod Bethune fought against racial discrimination and worked to improve the lives of African Americans through education, activism, and political advocacy. Her tireless efforts to advance the cause of black justice and equality have left an indelible mark on American history and continue to inspire generations of activists and leaders in the ongoing struggle for freedom and justice.

In the halls of education, Mary's legacy gleams,
A beacon of hope, in pursuit of dreams.
With passion and fervor, she paved the way,
For Black Americans, come what may.

As an advisor to Roosevelt, her voice was heard clear,
Advocating for rights, without any fear.
But if Mary were here, what mischief she'd brew,
With her wit and her wisdom, a force through and
through.

Perhaps she'd be schooling, with laughter in tow,
Teaching young minds, to always grow.
Or maybe advising, leaders today,
On equality and justice, in every which way.

Women of today, take heed of her tale,
With courage and grace, you'll never fail.
Embrace education, fight for your rights,
In Mary's footsteps, shine bright lights.

So let's raise a glass, to Mary's great name,
A trailblazer for women, in the hall of fame.
Let's honor her legacy, with joy and with pride,
And make her proud, with every stride!

Pauli Murray (1910 – 1985) was a pioneering civil rights activist, lawyer, author, and Episcopal priest who made significant contributions to the fight for black justice, equality, and freedom, as well as gender equality and LGBTQ+ rights. Murray's activism began in the 1930s when she became involved in the civil rights movement, working to challenge racial segregation and discrimination. She was a co-founder of the Congress of Racial Equality (CORE) and a key strategist in the fight against racial segregation in education. One of Murray's most notable achievements was her legal advocacy. In 1940, she applied to attend the University of North Carolina Law School but was denied admission because of her race. Murray's case, along with her groundbreaking legal arguments challenging segregation, laid the groundwork for the legal strategy used in the landmark Brown v. Board of Education Supreme Court case in 1954, which declared segregation in public schools unconstitutional. Murray was also a leading voice in the feminist movement, advocating for gender equality and women's rights. In 1966, she co-founded the National Organization for Women (NOW) and played a key role in shaping its agenda. As an openly gay woman, Murray was also a pioneer in the LGBTQ+ rights movement. She wrote extensively about her experiences as a queer person of color and advocated for the rights of LGBTQ+ individuals to live openly and without discrimination. Pauli Murray's legacy is one of courage, resilience, and unwavering dedication to justice. Her groundbreaking legal work, activism, and scholarship continue to inspire activists and advocates for civil rights, gender equality, and LGBTQ+ rights today.

In memory of Pauli Murray, let's sing a merry tune,
A trailblazer, a hero, shining brightly like the moon.
With a pen as sharp as any sword, she fought for what
was right,
Injustice trembled at her words, she was a beacon of
light.

A lawyer, writer, and priest, her talents knew no
bounds,
Breaking barriers, shattering norms, wherever she was
found.
Segregation, gender bias, she faced them head-on, no
jest,
Her courage and determination put bigotry to the test.

Co-founding The National Organization for Women
(NOW),
Her legacy, a testament to her might,
Empowering women, igniting flames, for equality to
ignite.
And as the first black woman priest, she blazed a
righteous trail,
Her spirit soaring high above, like a ship with full sail.

If Pauli walked among us now, what wonders would
she sow?

Perhaps leading marches, penning books, or teaching
us to grow.
Her voice would ring with wisdom, her laughter fill
the air,
A force for change, a guiding light, showing us all we
can dare.

So, let's honor her memory, with laughter, love, and
song,
And pledge to carry on her work, for justice to prolong.
For women of today, her spirit lights the way,
Emulate her strength, her grace, and make black
women proud each day.

Oscar Micheaux (1884 – 1951) was a pioneering African American filmmaker and author who made significant contributions to the fight for black justice, equality, and freedom, particularly through his groundbreaking films. Micheaux's career began in the early 20th century when he self-published his first novel, "The Conquest: The Story of a Negro Pioneer," in 1913. This marked the beginning of his prolific career as a writer and film-maker, during which he produced over 40 films and wrote several novels, many of which explored themes of race, identity, and social justice. One of Micheaux's most notable achievements was his role in breaking barriers in the film industry. At a time when Hollywood largely ignored the stories and experiences of African Americans, Micheaux founded the Micheaux Film and

Book Company in 1919, becoming the first African American to produce a feature-length film, "The Homesteader," in 1919. Micheaux's films often depicted the realities of black life in America, challenging stereotypes and giving voice to African Americans' experiences. He tackled issues such as racial discrimination, interracial relationships, and economic inequality, shedding light on the struggles and triumphs of black communities. In addition to his contributions to cinema, Micheaux was also a vocal advocate for black empowerment and civil rights. He used his platform as a filmmaker and author to speak out against racial injustice and advocate for social change, inspiring generations of African Americans to fight for equality and freedom. Oscar Micheaux's legacy is one of innovation, resilience, and unwavering dedication to justice. His pioneering work in film and literature paved the way for future generations of black filmmakers and artists and continues to inspire activists and advocates for civil rights today.

In memory of Oscar Micheaux, let's raise a cheer,
A filmmaker bold, with vision clear.
Over 40 films, he brought to the screen,
Tales of Black lives, vibrant and keen.

Challenging stereotypes, breaking the mold,
His stories were treasures, worth more than gold.
Despite financial woes, he pressed on strong,
His legacy echoes in cinematic song.

Now if Oscar were here, what would he do?
In today's world, with stories anew.
Perhaps he'd tackle streaming, with shows to binge,
Bringing Black voices to every screen's fringe.

Or maybe he'd venture into virtual space,
Creating immersive tales, in every place.
With technology's power, the sky's the limit,
His creativity would surely be infinite.

But let's not forget, beyond the screen,
The lessons he taught, the places he's been.
Men of today, take heed and learn,
From Micheaux's courage, let it burn.

Embrace your roots, stand tall and proud,
In every endeavor, let your voice be loud.
For in honoring his memory, we find,
The strength to uplift, the power to shine.

Bessie Coleman (1892 – 1926) was a pioneering African American aviator who made significant contributions to aviation and fought against racial discrimination and inequality in the early 20th century. Born to a poor family in Texas, Coleman faced significant obstacles in pursuing her dream of becoming a pilot due to racial and gender discrimination. Denied entry to aviation schools in the United States because of her race and gender, Coleman traveled to France in 1920 to earn her pilot's license. She became the first African American woman and the first Native American woman to hold a pilot's license. Coleman's achievements as a pilot made her an international sensation and an inspiration to

African Americans and women around the world. She performed in air shows and exhibitions, thrilling audiences with her daring stunts and aerial maneuvers. In addition to her contributions to aviation, Coleman used her platform to advocate for racial equality and civil rights. She refused to participate in air shows that excluded African American audiences and spoke out against segregation and discrimination in the aviation industry. Tragically, Bessie Coleman's life was cut short when she died in a plane crash during a test flight in 1926. However, her legacy as a trailblazer and pioneer in aviation continues to inspire generations of African American aviators and women in the fight for equality and freedom.

In memory of Bessie Coleman, let's take flight,
A pioneer in the sky, with wings so bright.
The first Black woman to earn her wings,
She soared above limits, like royalty's kings.

Born in a time of racial strife,
She faced discrimination in her quest for life.
But undeterred, she took to the air,
Breaking barriers with grace and flair.

Now imagine if Bessie were here today,
What soaring adventures would come her way?
Perhaps she'd zip through the clouds with ease,
Inspiring awe with every breeze.

Or maybe she'd teach, with patience and poise,
Guiding new aviators, both girls and boys.
Her legacy lives on, in every flight,
A beacon of hope, shining bright.

Women of today, take heed and see,
The courage of Bessie, the spirit so free.
Emulate her drive, her fearless heart,
And in your pursuits, play your part.

Break through barriers, reach for the sky,
Let your dreams soar, let your spirits fly.
For in honoring Bessie, we make a vow,
To uplift Black women, then and now.

Robert Smalls (1839 – 1915) was a remarkable African American leader and activist who made significant contributions to the fight for black justice, equality, and freedom during and after the Civil War. Born into slavery in South Carolina, Smalls worked as a laborer and eventually became a skilled sailor and ship pilot. In 1862, he orchestrated one of the most daring escapes from slavery when he commandeered a Confederate transport ship, the CSS Planter, and sailed it to Union-controlled waters, freeing himself, his family, and several other enslaved individuals. This audacious act of resistance brought Smalls national attention and made him a hero in the abolitionist movement. During the Civil War, Smalls served as a pilot for the Union Navy and became the first African American to command a U.S. Navy ship. He played a crucial role in numerous military engagements and reconnaissance missions, using his intimate knowledge of the coastal waters to assist the Union cause. After the war, Smalls continued his advocacy for civil rights and equality. He served as a delegate to the South Carolina Constitutional Convention of 1868, where he played a key role in drafting the state's new constitution, which guaranteed rights for African Americans, including the right to vote. Smalls went on to have a distinguished political career, serving in the South Carolina House of Representatives and later in the U.S. House of Representatives, where he fought for civil rights legislation and advocated for economic opportunities for African Americans. Throughout his life, Robert Smalls remained a tireless champion for justice and equality, using his position and influence to uplift his community and advance the cause of freedom for all. His courage, leadership, and dedication to the fight for black justice continue to inspire generations of activists and leaders today.

In memory of Robert Smalls, let's celebrate,
A hero of freedom, who defied his fate.
From enslaved to free, he sailed to his own tune,
A daring escape under the light of the moon.

Commandeering a ship, with courage and might,
He charted a course to freedom's bright light.
Delivering hope to Union's embrace,
With bravery etched on his determined face.

After the war, he didn't slow down,
A successful businessman, wearing no frown.
In politics, he made his voice heard,
For civil rights, he spread the word.
Now imagine if Robert were here today,
What feats of courage would come his way?
Perhaps he'd navigate through politics' sea,
Advocating for justice, for you and for me.

Or maybe he'd steer through business's tide,
Creating opportunities far and wide.
His legacy lives on, in every fight,
A beacon of hope, shining bright.

Men of today, take heed and learn,
From Robert Smalls, let your spirits churn.
Emulate his courage, his fearless heart,
And in your pursuits, play your part.

Break through barriers, chart your own course,
Let your voice ring out, with unyielding force.
For in honoring Robert, we make a vow,
To uplift Black men, then and now.

Maggie Lena Walker (1864 – 1934) was a trailblazing African American entrepreneur, community leader, and civil rights activist who made significant contributions to the fight for black justice, equality, and freedom. Walker's most notable achievement was her role as the first African American woman to charter and serve as president of a bank in the United States. In 1903, she founded the St. Luke Penny Savings Bank in Richmond, Virginia, which aimed to provide financial services and resources to African American communities. Under her leadership, the bank thrived and expanded, becoming a cornerstone of economic empowerment for black residents in Richmond and beyond. In addition to her work in banking, Walker was a prominent advocate for social and economic justice. She was deeply involved in the Independent Order of

St. Luke, a fraternal organization dedicated to the upliftment of African Americans, where she worked to provide financial assistance, educational opportunities, and social services to members of the community. Walker was also active in the struggle for civil rights and women's rights. She fought against racial segregation and discrimination, advocating for equal access to education, employment, and public accommodations. As a leader in the National Association of Colored Women (NACW), she worked to address social and political issues affecting African American women and families. Maggie Lena Walker's legacy is one of resilience, empowerment, and advocacy. Her pioneering achievements as a businesswoman and community leader laid the groundwork for future generations of African American entrepreneurs and activists, and her commitment to justice and equality continues to inspire individuals and communities today.

In Richmond town, where history blooms,
Lived Maggie Walker, with her savvy and booms.
She broke the mold, shattered the norm,
With wit and charm, she weathered the storm.

Maggie Lena, a woman of grace,
Led with style, set her own pace.
She chartered banks, broke barriers too,
A pioneer through and through.

With ink and pen, she wrote her name,
In golden letters, she claimed her fame.
St. Luke Penny Savings Bank, her pride,
Where dreams took flight, on a financial tide.

If Maggie were here, what would she do?
Perhaps host seminars, a financial guru.
Teaching women far and wide,
To stand tall, with financial pride.

In boardrooms, she'd take her seat,
With confidence, she'd compete.
Her laughter ringing, her wisdom shared,
A legacy of hope, beyond compare.

To women today, a call to arms,
Embrace your power, your many charms.
Like Maggie Lena, stand tall and strong,
In her footsteps, march along.

Empowerment is the key,
To unlock doors, set minds free.
Let Maggie's spirit guide your way,
To brighter tomorrows, come what may.

So, let's raise a toast, with joy and glee,
To Maggie Lena Walker, our legacy.
May her courage and grace forever endure,
In the hearts of women, strong and sure.

Charles Hamilton Houston (1895 – 1950) was a pioneering African American lawyer, educator, and civil rights activist who played a pivotal role in the legal battle against racial segregation and discrimination in the United States. Houston's most notable achievement was his strategic leadership in the campaign to dismantle segregation in public schools, culminating in the landmark Supreme Court case Brown v. Board of Education in 1954. As the first special counsel for the NAACP (National Association for the Advancement of Colored People), Houston developed a comprehensive legal strategy to challenge the "separate but equal" doctrine established by the Supreme Court in Plessy v. Ferguson (1896). He argued that segregation inherently denied African American children equal educational opportunities and was, therefore, unconstitutional. Houston's legal strategy focused on recruiting and training a new generation of African American lawyers, whom he referred to as "social engineers," to litigate cases challenging segregation and discrimination. Among his most famous proteges was Thurgood Marshall, who would later become the first African American Supreme Court Justice. Houston's efforts laid the groundwork for the eventual desegregation of American schools and paved the way for the broader civil rights movement of the 1950s and 1960s. His strategic brilliance and unwavering commitment to justice and equality continue to inspire generations of lawyers, activists, and scholars in the ongoing struggle for civil rights and social justice.

In the annals of justice, a hero stands tall,
Charles Hamilton Houston, heeding justice's call.
With wit and wisdom, he fought the fight,
Dismantling segregation, with all his might.

A mentor to Marshall, a beacon of light,
In the courtroom battles, he'd always ignite.
With eloquence and strategy, he paved the way,
For equality to dawn, come what may.

If Charles were here, what would he do?
Perhaps penning briefs, with a witty hue.
Arguing cases, with passion and flair,
Seeking justice, beyond compare.

In legal forums, he'd take his stand,
Championing rights, across the land.
His laughter ringing, his intellect shared,
A legacy of courage, beyond compare.

To men today, a message rings clear,
Embrace your power, banish fear.
Like Charles Hamilton, stand tall and proud,
In his footsteps, march along, unbowed.

Equality is the mission,
To dismantle barriers, with precision.
Let Charles's spirit guide your way,
To brighter tomorrows, come what may.

So let's raise a cheer, with joy and glee,
To Charles Hamilton Houston, our legacy.
May his courage and wisdom forever endure,
In the hearts of men, strong and sure.

Ella Baker (1903 – 1986) was a pioneering African American civil rights activist and organizer who made significant contributions to the fight for black justice, equality, and freedom during the mid-20th century. Baker's most notable achievement was her leadership in grassroots organizing and her role in fostering a more participatory and decentralized approach to civil rights activism. She played a key role in several major civil rights organizations, including the NAACP (National Association for the Advancement of Colored People) and the Southern Christian Leadership Conference (SCLC). Baker is perhaps best known for her work with the Student Nonviolent Coordinating Committee

(SNCC), which she helped found in 1960. As an advisor and mentor to young activists in SNCC, Baker emphasized the importance of empowering ordinary people to lead their own struggles for justice and equality. She believed in the power of collective action and encouraged SNCC members to organize from the grassroots rather than relying on charismatic leaders. Baker's philosophy of grassroots organizing and participatory democracy had a profound impact on the civil rights movement. It helped shift the focus from top-down leadership to grassroots mobilization. Her leadership and mentorship paved the way for the emergence of a new generation of activist leaders, many of whom went on to play prominent roles in the movement. Throughout her life, Ella Baker remained committed to the fight for justice and equality for all people, regardless of race or background. Her legacy as a tireless advocate for grassroots organizing and social change continues to inspire activists and organizers around the world in the ongoing struggle for civil rights and social justice.

In the annals of history, a name we hold dear,
Ella Baker, a force without fear.
Behind the scenes, she toiled away,
Empowering activists in her own special way.

With a twinkle in her eye and a heart so bold,
She founded movements, stories untold.
The Southern Christian Leadership Conference (SCLC)
And the Student Nonviolent
Coordinating Committee (SNCC), her legacy grand,
A trailblazer of change in a divided land.

But what if she were here with us now,
With wisdom to share, with lessons to endow?
Perhaps she'd be rallying, organizing still,
Fighting for justice with unyielding will.

In the halls of power, her voice would ring clear,
Demanding equality, erasing every fear.
Or perhaps in communities, she'd sow seeds of change,
Inspiring women, breaking free from every chain.

For Ella showed us what it means to stand tall,
To answer the call, to heed the call.
So let us, women of today, take her lead,
Emulate her grace, her strength, her creed.

Let us march forward, with heads held high,
Making black women proud as we reach for the sky.
For in our hands lies the power to create,
A world where justice and love shall never abate.

Diane Judith Nash (born May 15, 1938) is a prominent African American civil rights activist known for her pivotal role in the fight for black justice, equality, and freedom during the 1960s. Nash's most notable achievement was her leadership in the Nashville sit-ins, which played a crucial role in desegregating lunch counters in Nashville, Tennessee. In 1960, she helped organize and coordinate sit-ins at downtown lunch counters, where African Americans were refused service due to segregation policies. Nash's strategic planning and commitment to nonviolent protest were instrumental in the success of the sit-ins, which drew national attention to the injustice of segregation and inspired similar protests across the country. Following the success of the sit-ins, Nash became a leader in the Freedom Riders movement, which aimed to challenge segregation on interstate buses and in bus terminals. She was a key organizer of the Freedom Rides and participated in several dangerous and violent protests, including one in Montgomery, Alabama, where she was arrested and spent time in jail. Nash's activism extended beyond the Freedom Rides. She played a key role in organizing voter registration drives and other civil rights campaigns throughout the 1960s. Her commitment to nonviolent direct action and unwavering dedication to justice and equality made her a respected and influential leader in the civil rights movement. Diane Nash's legacy as a fearless activist and organizer continues to inspire generations of activists and advocates for social justice. Her contributions to the civil rights movement helped bring about significant advances in the fight for black justice, equality, and freedom, and her legacy serves as a reminder of the power of grassroots organizing and nonviolent resistance in the struggle for justice and equality.

In the heart of the South, where dreams take flight,
Stood a woman with courage, her spirit alight.
Diane Nash, with fire in her eyes,
A leader, a hero, under Southern skies.

With sit-ins and freedom rides, she took a stand,
Challenging segregation, with a firm hand.
The Freedom Riders' success, owed much to her,
A founding member of the Student Nonviolent
Coordinating Committee (SNCC), her influence sure.

But if Diane were active today,
What mischief, what magic, what games would she
play?
Perhaps she'd organize, with passion and zest,
Rallying women, to rise up and protest.

In boardrooms and classrooms, her voice would
resound,
Fighting for justice, breaking barriers down.
Or maybe she'd dance, with joy and with glee,
Celebrating victories, wild and free.

So let us, women of today, take her cue,
Embrace her spirit, her courage so true.
Let's stand tall, let's make our voices heard,
And make black women proud with every word.

For Diane Nash showed us what it means to fight,
To stand up for what's just, with all of our might.
So let's honor her legacy, let's carry her flame,
And make her proud.

Peter Salem (c. 1750 – 1816) was a notable African American soldier who fought for American independence during the Revolutionary War and made significant contributions to the fight for black justice, equality, and freedom. Salem's most notable achievement occurred during the Battle of Bunker Hill on June 17, 1775, where he distinguished himself for his bravery and skill as a soldier. During the battle, Salem served as a member of the Massachusetts militia, fighting alongside other patriots against British forces. It is reported that Salem was credited with fatally shooting British Marine Major John Pitcairn, a significant achievement that helped boost morale among American forces. Salem's bravery at the Battle of Bunker Hill earned him recognition and praise from his fellow soldiers and officers, as well as from prominent leaders of the American Revolution, including General George Washington. After the Revolutionary War, Salem continued to advocate for black justice and freedom by petitioning the Massachusetts legislature for a pension, which was eventually granted to him in recognition of his military service. Peter Salem's courage and sacrifice during the Revolutionary War exemplify the significant contributions of African Americans to the fight for American independence. His legacy serves as a reminder of the important role that black soldiers played in securing freedom and equality for all Americans.

In the heat of battle, with muskets ablaze,
Stood Peter Salem, his courage a blaze.
At Bunker Hill, he fought with might,
A hero in the midst of the fight.

With steady hand and steady aim,
He took down Pitcairn, etching his name.
A soldier brave, in history's scroll,
His bravery echoed from pole to pole.

But if Peter were here with us now,
What mischief, what laughter, what tales would he
plow?
Perhaps he'd be a chef, cooking with flair,
Delighting friends with dishes beyond compare.

Or maybe a teacher, with wisdom to share,
Inspiring young minds with stories rare.
Or perhaps a comedian, with jokes that delight,
Spreading laughter and joy, morning to night.

For Peter Salem showed us what it means to be bold,
To face adversity, with a spirit untold.
So let us, men of today, take his lead,
Emulate his courage, his strength, his creed.

Let's stand tall, let's make our mark,
And make black men proud with every spark.
For in our hands lies the power to shine,
And honor heroes like Peter, for all time.

James Armistead Lafayette (c. 1748 – c. 1830) was an enslaved African American who served as a spy for the Continental Army during the American Revolutionary War, making significant contributions to the fight for American independence and, indirectly, to the cause of black justice, equality, and freedom. Armistead's most notable achievement occurred during his service as a double agent, working as a spy for the Marquis de Lafayette, a French military officer who served as a major general in the Continental Army. Armistead posed as a runaway slave seeking refuge with the British forces, earning their trust and gaining access to valuable information about British troop movements and plans. Armistead's intelligence gathering was instrumental in several key battles, including the decisive Battle of Yorktown in 1781, where British General Cornwallis was forced to surrender, effectively ending the war. After the Revolutionary War, Armistead petitioned the Virginia General Assembly for his freedom, citing his valuable service to the Continental Army. In 1787, the assembly granted him his freedom, and he adopted the last name Lafayette in honor of the French general who had befriended him during the war. James Armistead Lafayette's bravery and ingenuity as a spy played a significant role in the American victory over the British and helped secure independence for the United States. His contributions to the Revolutionary War and his pursuit of freedom and justice exemplify the important role that African Americans played in the fight for American independence and in advancing the cause of black justice, equality, and freedom.

In days of old, in tales untold,
Lies a hero both brave and bold.
James Armistead, his name we hail,
A double agent, never frail.

From shackles bound, he rose on high,
Sought freedom's call, across the sky.
In shadows deep, his wit did dance,
Spying for freedom, in every glance.

With cunning schemes and stealthy stride,
He slipped through ranks, with patriot's pride.
To General Lafayette, he brought insight,
A key to winning the Yorktown fight.

Now, if James walked among us today,
In modern times, what would he say?
Perhaps he'd stand for truth and right,
Encouraging all to join the fight.

Not with swords or muskets loud,
But with wisdom's pen, in justice proud.
For men of every creed and hue,
To stand as one, in courage true.

So let us honor James's name,
With laughter, love, and hearts aflame.
And in his footsteps, let us trod,
Making proud every black man of God.

Prince Whipple (c. 1750—after 1796) was an African American enslaved man who gained recognition for his service during the American Revolutionary War. He fought for American independence and indirectly contributed to the cause of black justice, equality, and freedom. Whipple's most notable achievement occurred during the Revolutionary War when he served as an aide-de-camp to General William Whipple, a signer of the Declaration of Independence and a military leader in the Continental Army. Prince Whipple fought alongside General Whipple in several key battles, including the pivotal Battle of Saratoga in 1777.

Whipple's service as an aide-de-camp demonstrated the significant contributions of African Americans to the American Revolutionary War effort. Despite being enslaved, Whipple risked his life to fight for American independence, embodying the ideals of freedom and equality espoused by the Revolutionary Movement. After the Revolutionary War, Whipple's status as an enslaved man remained unchanged, and there was limited information available about his life following the war. However, his bravery and service during the Revolutionary War serve as a reminder of the important role that African Americans played in securing independence for the United States and in advancing the cause of black justice, equality, and freedom.

In days of yore, a tale of lore,
Of Prince Whipple, we adore.
Beside his master, bold and true,
He fought for freedom, through and through.

Amidst the fray, his spirit soared,
Crossing rivers, battles roared.
With General Washington by his side,
He faced the storm, with courage wide.

If Prince Whipple walked our streets today,
In modern times, what would he say?
Perhaps he'd teach, with wisdom's grace,
That unity and love must embrace.

He'd stand for justice, loud and clear,
Dispelling darkness, bringing cheer.
For men of all, in every land,
To join as one, with heart in hand.

So let us honor Prince's name,
With joy, with laughter, without shame.
And in his footsteps, let us stride,
Making proud every black man's pride.

Wentworth Cheswell (1746 – 1817) was a notable African American patriot, teacher, and public servant who made significant contributions to the fight for black justice, equality, and freedom during the American Revolutionary War and beyond. Cheswell's most notable achievement was his service as a prominent political leader and civic figure in New Hampshire during the Revolutionary War era. In addition to his work as a teacher and educator, Cheswell served as a town constable, a selectman, and an assessor in the town of Newmarket, New Hampshire. He was also elected as a delegate to the New Hampshire Provincial

Assembly in 1775, making him one of the first African Americans to hold elected office in colonial America. During the American Revolutionary War, Cheswell served as a member of the New Hampshire militia and fought alongside his fellow patriots in defense of American independence. He participated in the Battle of Saratoga in 1777, a decisive American victory that helped turn the tide of the war in favor of the Patriots. In addition to his military and political service, Cheswell was also active in his local community and church, advocating for social and economic justice for African Americans and other marginalized groups. He was known for his integrity, leadership, and commitment to the principles of equality and freedom. Wentworth Cheswell's contributions to the American Revolutionary War and his leadership in the fight for justice and equality serve as a reminder of the important role that African Americans played in the struggle for American independence and in shaping the nation's history. His legacy continues to inspire generations of activists and advocates for civil rights and social justice.

In the heart of New Hampshire, a man of great renown,
Wentworth Cheswell, the toast of the town!
As leader, judge, and soldier bold,
His legacy shines brighter than gold.

In the Revolutionary War, he took his stand,
A brave African American, with sword in hand.
Through battles fierce, he fought with might,
For freedom's cause, he led the fight.

Elected to office, a historic feat,
Wentworth Cheswell, oh, what a treat!
The first of his kind, breaking through the divide,
A beacon of hope, for equality's tide.

If he were here today, what would he do?
Lead with wisdom, and laughter too!
Perhaps he'd be a voice for change,
Injustice's foe, he'd surely arrange.

In a world full of strife, his example shines bright,
Men of today, take heed, and take flight!
Emulate his courage, his strength, and his grace,
Make black men proud, in every place.

So let's raise a toast to Wentworth Cheswell's name,
A hero of history, his legacy aflame!
With sweet laughter and joy, let's honor his quest,
And strive for a future where all are blessed.

Martin Delany (1812 – 1885) was a pioneering African American abolitionist, journalist, physician, and political leader who made significant contributions to the fight for black justice, equality, and freedom during the 19th century. Delany's most notable achievement was his work as an influential leader in the abolitionist movement. He advocated for the immediate emancipation of enslaved African Americans and worked tirelessly to end the institution of slavery in the United States. Delany was an outspoken critic of the colonization movement, which advocated for the resettlement of freed slaves in Africa and instead argued for full citizenship and equal rights for African Americans in the United States. As a journalist, Delany used his platform to amplify the voices of African Americans and advocate for social and political change. He published several newspapers, including "The Mystery" and "The North Star," which provided a forum for discussions on abolitionism, racial equality, and black empowerment.

Delany was also a prominent leader in the fight for black civil rights and political representation. He was one of the first African Americans to be admitted to Harvard Medical School, although he ultimately did not graduate due to racial discrimination. Delany also served as a recruiter for the Union Army during the Civil War, advocating for the enlistment of African American soldiers and fighting for their right to serve in combat roles. After the Civil War, Delany continued to be active in the struggle for civil rights and equality. He became involved in politics and was a delegate to several national conventions of the Republican Party, where he advocated for policies to advance the rights and interests of African Americans. Martin Delany's legacy as a pioneering abolitionist, journalist, and political leader continues to inspire generations of activists and advocates for black justice, equality, and freedom. His contributions to the abolitionist movement and the fight for civil rights helped lay the groundwork for the advancements in racial equality that followed in the years to come.

In days of old, a man so bold,
With courage fierce, his story's told.
Martin Delany, a name renowned,
In history's pages, forever crowned.

An abolitionist, brave and true,
His voice rang out, clear as the blue.
A journalist, he penned the fight,
With words that soared, like birds in flight.

A physician skilled, with healing hands,
He tended wounds in troubled lands.
But it's his role in the Union Army's fray,
That shines so bright, to this very day.

A major's rank, he proudly bore,
Amongst the troops, he fought for more.
Enlisting blacks, with fervent zeal,
His courage forged a mighty steel.

Now, if Delany walked this earth anew,
What would he do? What would ensue?
Perhaps he'd march, in rights' crusade,
Or pen fierce words, with ink-drenched blade.

He'd stand for justice, bold and strong,
His legacy echoing, loud and long.
To men today, a lesson clear,
In Delany's footsteps, they should steer.

Embrace the fight, for what is right,
With courage strong, and hearts alight.
Make black men proud, in every way,
Let Delany's spirit guide today.

William Harvey Carney (1840 – 1908) was a courageous African American soldier who made significant contributions to the fight for black justice, equality, and freedom during the American Civil War. Carney's most notable achievement occurred during the Battle of Fort Wagner in 1863. Serving as a member of the 54th Massachusetts Infantry Regiment, one of the first African American units to be organized in the Union Army, Carney participated in the assault on the Confederate-held fort in South Carolina. Despite sustaining serious injuries, including multiple gunshot wounds, Carney refused to retreat and continued to carry the American flag forward, refusing to let it touch the ground. His actions inspired his fellow soldiers and demonstrated his unwavering commitment to the cause of freedom and equality. For his bravery and heroism at Fort Wagner, Carney became the first African American to be awarded the Medal of Honor, the nation's highest military honor. His selfless actions in battle exemplified the courage and sacrifice of African American soldiers fighting for their own liberation and the freedom of their fellow citizens. After the war, Carney continued to advocate for civil rights and equality for African Americans. He was active in veterans' organizations and became a prominent figure in the African American community, serving as an inspiration and role model for generations to come. William Harvey Carney's legacy as a hero of the Civil War and a champion for black justice and equality continues to inspire Americans today. His courageous actions on the battlefield and his lifelong commitment to freedom and justice serve as a reminder of the enduring struggle for equality and the contributions of African Americans to the nation's history.

In tales of valor, let's not forget,
William Carney, with no regret.
A hero bold, in battle's blaze,
His courage shining, through the haze.

At Fort Wagner, he made his stand,
The Union flag, in his brave hand.
Though wounded sore, he held it high,
With steadfast spirit, reaching the sky.

The Medal of Honor, he rightly earned,
For bravery that brightly burned.
But what if Carney walked today,
In modern times, what would he say?

Perhaps he'd teach, with wisdom's light,
To stand for truth, and what is right.
To carry on, despite the odds,
And never yield, to fearful nods.

In fields of justice, he'd surely roam,
His voice a trumpet, calling home.
To men today, a message clear,
In Carney's footsteps, boldly steer.

With honor high, and hearts aflame,
Make black men proud, and stake your claim.
For like Carney, in days of yore,
We carry on, forevermore.

Susie King Taylor (1848 – 1912) was an African American educator, nurse, and activist who made significant contributions to the fight for black justice, equality, and freedom during and after the American Civil War. Taylor's most notable achievement was her service as a nurse and teacher during the Civil War. Born into slavery in Georgia, she gained her freedom at the age of 14 and joined a Union Army regiment as a laundress and nurse. Taylor was the only African American woman to publish a memoir of her experiences during the Civil War, titled "Reminiscences of My Life in Camp with the 33d United States Colored Troops, Late 1st S.C. Volunteers." In it, she detailed her experiences caring for wounded soldiers and educating

African American children in contraband camps, where escaped slaves sought refuge behind Union lines. Taylor's work as a nurse and teacher in the contraband camps was instrumental in providing education and medical care to newly liberated African Americans and their families. She played a crucial role in advancing the cause of black justice and equality by empowering formerly enslaved individuals through education and healthcare. After the Civil War, Taylor continued her advocacy for civil rights and social justice. She became involved in the women's suffrage movement and worked to advance the rights of African American women and girls. Susie King Taylor's legacy as a nurse, teacher, and activist serves as a testament to the resilience and courage of African American women during the Civil War era. Her contributions to the fight for black justice, equality, and freedom continue to inspire activists and advocates for civil rights and social justice today.

In the annals of time, there's a tale quite profound,
Of a lady named Susie, whose heart knew no bound.
With courage she marched, in the Civil War's fray,
As a nurse for the Union, come what may.

In camp, she tended to the wounded and sore,
With kindness and care, she gave all she bore.
Through battles and hardships, her spirit stood tall,
A beacon of hope amidst war's dark thrall.

But Susie King Taylor wasn't just a nurse at heart,
She taught newly freed souls, she played a vital part.
In educating minds, she sowed seeds of light,
Guiding toward knowledge, banishing the night.

Now imagine if Susie were here by our side,
In this modern world, where dreams often collide.
Perhaps she'd be teaching, inspiring anew,
Her wisdom and grace, a timeless debut.

In classrooms or forums, her voice would resound,
Empowering others to stand firm and astound.
For women today, her example rings clear,
To strive for greatness, to banish all fear.

So, let's raise a toast to Susie, her legacy grand,
A heroine true in our nation's own land.
May her spirit endure, may her story inspire,
And may black women rise, their hearts set on fire.

George Washington Carver (1860s—1943) was a prominent African American scientist, educator, and inventor who made significant contributions to agricultural science and fought for black justice, equality, and freedom during the late 19th and early 20th centuries. Carver's most notable achievement was his groundbreaking work in agricultural science, particularly his research into crop rotation and soil conservation techniques. He developed hundreds of new uses for crops such as peanuts, soybeans, and sweet potatoes, helping to improve the economic prospects of Southern farmers, many of whom were African American. Carver's research and innovations had a profound impact on American agriculture and helped to alleviate poverty and hunger in the rural South. He advocated for sustainable farming practices and emphasized the importance of education and scientific research in improving the lives of African Americans and other marginalized communities. In addition to his scientific achievements, Carver was a vocal advocate for racial equality and social justice. He believed in the power of education to uplift African Americans and fought against racial discrimination and segregation throughout his life. Carver's work as a scientist and educator helped to challenge stereotypes and misconceptions about African Americans and paved the way for future generations of African American scientists and scholars. His legacy as a pioneering agricultural scientist and civil rights advocate continues to inspire people around the world to this day.

In fields of green, where crops abound,
Lived a man named George, both wise and sound.
With peanuts and spuds, he'd dance and prance,
Inventing and innovating, taking a chance.

From soil to sky, his mind did roam,
Finding solutions far from home.
With sweet potatoes and legumes in hand,
He crafted marvels across the land.

But imagine if George were here today,
In this world of hustle and fray.
Perhaps he'd be tilling in his lab,
Cooking up ideas, a scientific fab!

He'd whip up potions, concoctions galore,
Solving problems we hadn't seen before.
From eco-friendly fuel to food that's divine,
George's inventions would surely shine.

So, men of today, take heed and learn,
From this scientist, it's time to discern.
With perseverance and a curious eye,
You, too, can reach for the sky so high.

Make George Carver proud, let his legacy gleam,
Innovate, create, and dare to dream.
For black men everywhere, let it be said,
You're walking the path that George once tread.

Mae Jemison (born October 17, 1956) is an American engineer, physician, and former NASA astronaut who made history as the first African American woman to travel to space. Jemison's most notable achievement was her journey aboard the Space Shuttle Endeavour in September 1992, during mission STS-47. As a mission specialist, she conducted scientific experiments on bone cell research and fluid dynamics while orbiting the Earth, becoming a symbol of inspiration and breaking barriers in the field of space exploration. In addition to her groundbreaking career as an astronaut, Jemison is also a dedicated advocate for diversity in

STEM (science, technology, engineering, and mathematics) fields and a vocal proponent of social justice and equality. She has worked tirelessly to promote STEM education, particularly among underrepresented minority groups, and to encourage young people to pursue their passions in science and exploration. Jemison's achievements have earned her numerous awards and honors, including induction into the National Women's Hall of Fame and the International Space Hall of Fame. She continues to inspire individuals around the world with her pioneering spirit, commitment to excellence, and dedication to advancing the cause of black justice, equality, and freedom.

In a galaxy not so far away,
Mae Jemison soared on her way.
With Endeavour as her trusty steed,
She blazed a trail, fulfilling every need.

A doctor turned astronaut, oh what a feat!
Cornell's halls once echoed her heartbeat.
Peace Corps called, she answered with glee,
Then off to NASA, her destiny.

But wait, there's more to this tale,
Than just a journey on a cosmic sail.
For Mae, the stars were just the start,
Her impact on Earth, a work of art.

With The Jemison Group, she paved the way,
A tech consultant, guiding night and day.
Inspiring speeches, igniting STEM's fire,
Her voice, a beacon, rising higher and higher.

In classrooms and labs, her legacy gleams,
Igniting young minds, fulfilling dreams.
For women of today, her path to follow,
Breaking barriers, with courage to swallow.

So let's raise a cheer, for Mae Jemison bright,
A shining star in our cosmic sight.
Her laughter echoes through the universe's hum,
A beacon of hope, for generations to come.

Lewis Howard Latimer (1848 – 1928) was an African American inventor, draftsman, and engineer who made significant contributions to technological innovation during the late 19th and early 20th centuries. His achievements helped to advance the cause of black justice, equality, and freedom. Latimer's most notable achievement was improving the practical application of the electric light bulb. He played a key role in developing and patenting the carbon filament, which made electric lighting more efficient and affordable. His innovations were crucial in making electric lighting accessible to a wider population and revolutionized industries and daily life around the world. In addition to his contributions to electric lighting, Latimer was also an accomplished draftsman and engineer. He worked closely with notable inventors such as Alexander Graham Bell and Thomas Edison, providing technical expertise and helping to bring their inventions to fruition. Latimer's achievements were particularly significant in the context of racial inequality and discrimination in the United States during his lifetime. As an African American inventor and engineer, he faced numerous challenges and barriers to success, but his perseverance, talent, and dedication allowed him to overcome these obstacles and make lasting contributions to science and technology. Latimer's legacy continues to inspire generations of inventors, engineers, and innovators, particularly those from underrepresented minority groups. His pioneering work in the field of electric lighting and his commitment to excellence serve as a reminder of the importance of diversity and inclusion in driving progress and innovation.

In a world of sparks and wires so bright,
Lives a man who brought us light,
Lewis Howard Latimer, oh what a sight,
Invention's champion, with all his might!

With Edison, he danced in the glow,
A symphony of ideas, a dazzling show,
Bulbs and wires, they did bestow,
A brighter world, for all to know.

But now, if Lewis were still around,
Inventor extraordinaire, forever renowned,
Perhaps he'd tinker with gadgets profound,
In the digital age, his genius unbound.

He'd Skype with Bell, on the telephone line,
Share jokes and wisdom, oh so fine,
"Keep inventing," he'd say, "it's a sign,
Of progress and hope, for all mankind!"

To the men of today, a lesson to heed,
From Latimer's legacy, take the lead,
Innovation, perseverance, at top speed,
Make history proud, fulfill the creed.

So, let's raise a toast, to Latimer's might,
His legacy shines, forever bright,
Inventors, dreamers, take flight,
And make black men proud, with all your might!

Garrett Morgan (1877 – 1963) was an African American inventor and entrepreneur who made significant contributions to technological innovation and safety during the early 20th century. His achievements helped advance the cause of black justice, equality, and freedom. Morgan's most notable invention was the three-position traffic signal, patented in 1923. This traffic signal, which featured a warning light to signal when the traffic signal was about to change, greatly improved safety at intersections and became the basis for modern traffic signal systems used worldwide. In addition to his work on traffic safety, Morgan invented the safety hood, also known as the gas mask, in 1914. Originally designed to protect workers from inhaling toxic fumes in industrial settings, the safety hood later gained widespread use during World War I to protect soldiers from chemical warfare agents. Morgan's inventions were particularly significant in the context of racial inequality and discrimination in the United States during his lifetime. As an African American inventor and entrepreneur, he faced numerous challenges and barriers to success, but his ingenuity and perseverance allowed him to overcome these obstacles and make lasting contributions to public safety and technological innovation. Morgan's legacy continues to inspire generations of inventors, engineers, and innovators, particularly those from underrepresented minority groups. His pioneering work in the field of traffic safety and his commitment to excellence serve as a reminder of the importance of diversity and inclusion in driving progress and innovation.

In the annals of safety, a hero stands tall,
Garrett Morgan's inventions, he gave it his all,
Gas mask and traffic light, answering the call,
For public safety, he gave his all!

With a wink and a smile, he'd tinker away,
Inventing solutions, come what may,
If Morgan were here, what would he say?
"Keep innovating, every single day!"

Perhaps in our era of pollution and haze,
He'd craft devices to clear the airways,
Or in traffic jams, his wisdom would blaze,
Navigating chaos, with innovative craze!

To the men of today, let Morgan inspire,
His legacy burns, a relentless fire,
With perseverance and grit, aim higher and higher,
Make history proud, be the change you desire!

So here's to Garrett, with a nod and a cheer,
His brilliance shines, oh so clear,
Inventors, dreamers, lend us your ear,
Make black men proud, let innovation steer!

Louis Armstrong (1901 – 1971), often referred to as "Satchmo" or "Pops," was an iconic African American jazz trumpeter, composer, and singer whose contributions to music transformed the genre and helped to break down racial barriers in American society. Armstrong's most notable achievement was his pioneering role in the development of jazz music. His innovative trumpet playing and unique vocal style revolutionized the genre, influencing countless musicians and shaping the course of American music history. Armstrong's virtuosic improvisation, rhythmic innovations, and distinctive gravelly voice made him one of the most influential and beloved figures in jazz. In addition to his musical achievements, Armstrong was a vocal advocate for racial equality and social justice. Throughout his career, he faced discrimination and racism, but he used his platform and influence to speak out against injustice and promote racial harmony. He famously criticized the federal government's response to the Little Rock Nine crisis in 1957, expressing his outrage at the treatment of African American students attempting to desegregate a high school in Arkansas. Armstrong's music also helped to break down racial barriers. His performances with integrated bands and collaborations with white musicians helped to bridge racial divides and challenge stereotypes about African American artists. His international fame and popularity as a jazz ambassador further contributed to the recognition and appreciation of African American culture around the world. Louis Armstrong's legacy as a musical innovator and civil rights advocate continues to inspire musicians and activists today. His groundbreaking contributions to jazz music and his unwavering commitment to fighting for black justice, equality, and freedom have left an indelible mark on American culture and society.

In the land of jazz, where melodies dance,
There lived a man, with trumpet in hand.
Louis Armstrong, his name did ring,
With tunes so sweet, they made hearts sing.

Pioneering he was, in music's embrace,
Crafting rhythms with skill and grace.
His trumpet blared, like a joyful call,
Bringing smiles to faces, big and small.

Now if Louis were here, what would he do?
Perhaps still blowing tunes, fresh and new.
In a world of strife, his music would soar,
Bringing peace and joy, forevermore.

Men of today, take heed and learn,
From Louis' legacy, let it burn.
With charisma and style, and a jazz-filled sound,
Make black men proud, let their greatness abound.

So, pick up your horns, and play with glee,
Emulate Louis, and set your spirit free.
For in the rhythm of life, let your soul take flight,
And make the world brighter, with your own jazz
delight!

Carter G. Woodson (1875 – 1950) was an African American historian, author, and educator who made significant contributions to the study and promotion of black history and culture in the United States. His achievements helped to advance the cause of black justice, equality, and freedom. Woodson's most notable achievement was his pioneering efforts to establish the field of African American history as a legitimate area of scholarly inquiry. In 1915, he founded the Association for the Study of Negro Life and History (now known as the Association for the Study of African American Life and History) to promote the study and dissemination of information about black history and culture. He also established the Journal of Negro History in 1916, providing a platform for the publication of research on

African American history. In 1926, Woodson initiated the celebration of Negro History Week, which later evolved into Black History Month. This annual observance aimed to highlight the contributions and achievements of African Americans throughout history and to promote greater awareness and understanding of black history and culture. Woodson's advocacy for the study of black history was rooted in his belief that knowledge of one's own history and culture is essential for achieving racial pride, self-respect, and equality. He argued that African Americans should take an active role in reclaiming and preserving their own history rather than relying on others to tell their story. Through his writing, teaching, and activism, Woodson challenged prevailing racial stereotypes and promoted a more inclusive and accurate understanding of American history. His efforts helped to lay the foundation for the development of African American studies as a recognized academic discipline and contributed to the broader struggle for civil rights and social justice. Carter G. Woodson's legacy as a pioneering historian and educator continues to inspire scholars, educators, and activists today. His commitment to documenting and preserving the history and culture of African Americans has left an indelible mark on American society and has helped to advance the cause of black justice, equality, and freedom.

In the annals of history, there stands a man so bright,
Carter G. Woodson, a beacon in the night.
Known as the "Father of Black History" with pride,
He opened doors of knowledge, no longer to hide.

With pen in hand, he chronicled the tales,
Of African Americans, their victories and travails.
From fields to classrooms, he paved the way,
For truth and understanding to have their say.

Negro History Week, his brilliant creation,
Evolved into a month-long celebration.
A legacy of honor, culture, and grace,
A vibrant tapestry of our shared human race.

But what if old Carter were here today?
What mischief and wisdom would come his way?
Perhaps he'd be tweeting with scholarly wit,
Or lecturing crowds with a humorous skit.

In cafes and libraries, he'd hold court,
With anecdotes and facts of every sort.
Encouraging all to seek knowledge's light,
And celebrate Black history with all their might.

So, men of today, take heed and beware,
Emulate Woodson, with style and flair.
In honoring the past, we shape our fate,
And make Black men proud, it's never too late.

So, raise a glass to Carter, his legacy true,
And may we all learn from the things he knew.
For in his footsteps, we find our way,
To a brighter tomorrow, come what may!

Bessie Smith (1894 – 1937) was a renowned African American blues singer who achieved fame during the 1920s and 1930s, becoming one of the most influential and successful performers of her time. While she didn't engage in explicit activism, her achievements and contributions helped to advance the cause of black justice, equality, and freedom in several ways. Smith's most notable achievement was her groundbreaking career as a blues singer. Known as the "Empress of the Blues," she recorded hundreds of songs that captured the experiences and emotions of African Americans during the early 20th century. Her powerful voice, emotive delivery, and commanding stage presence made her one of the most celebrated and highest-paid entertainers of her era. Through her music, Smith addressed themes of love, loss, hardship, and resilience. She provided a voice for the African American community and reflected on the struggles and triumphs of black life in America. In doing so, she helped to challenge stereotypes and break down racial barriers in the music industry. Smith's success also contributed to greater economic empowerment and social mobility for African American artists. As one of the first African American women to achieve widespread fame and financial success in the music industry, she paved the way for future generations of black performers and helped elevate the status of African American music and culture in American society. While Smith's contributions to black justice, equality, and freedom were primarily cultural rather than political, her impact on the music industry and popular culture helped to challenge racial stereotypes and promote greater understanding and appreciation of African American art and expression. Her legacy as a pioneering blues singer and cultural icon continues to inspire artists and audiences around the world, and her music remains a powerful testament to the resilience and creativity of the African American experience.

In the sultry world of blues, there reigned a queen,
Bessie Smith, with a voice like you've never seen.
The "Empress of the Blues," with a crown of soul,
Her melodies could make a heartache whole.

From juke joints to theaters, she'd command the stage,
With every note, she'd ignite a fiery rage.
Paving the way for generations to come,
Her legacy shines bright, never to succumb.

But what if dear Bessie were still here today?
What mischief and melodies would come her way?
Perhaps she'd be belting out tunes on TikTok,
Or jamming with Beyoncé down by the dock.

In a world of auto-tune and synthesized beats,
She'd remind us all of the power in our feats.
With a wink and a smile, she'd sing from the heart,
Inspiring women to make their own art.

So, ladies of today, take note and beware,
Emulate Bessie, with style and flair.
In honoring her spirit, we find our own voice,
And make Black women proud, it's our own choice.

So, raise a glass to Bessie, her legacy true,
And may we all learn from the things she knew.
For in her melodies, we find our way,
To a brighter tomorrow, come what may!

DUKE ELLINGTON

Duke Ellington (1899 – 1974) was an iconic African American composer, pianist, and bandleader who made significant contributions to the world of jazz music and fought for black justice, equality, and freedom through his artistic endeavors. Ellington's most notable achievement was his groundbreaking work as a composer and bandleader. He composed thousands of pieces of music over his career, including jazz standards such as "Mood Indigo," "Take the 'A' Train," and "Sophisticated Lady." His innovative compositions and arrangements helped to redefine the genre of jazz and established him as one of the most influential musicians of the 20th century. As a bandleader, Ellington led one of the most renowned and long-lasting jazz orchestras in history, the Duke Ellington Orchestra. Known for its virtuosic musicianship, sophisticated arrangements, and dynamic performances, the orchestra became synonymous with the Harlem Renaissance, a cultural and artistic movement that celebrated African American culture and identity during the 1920s and 1930s. Through his music, Ellington addressed themes of African American identity, pride, and resilience, providing a voice for the African American community and challenging racial stereotypes and discrimination. His compositions often celebrated the rich cultural heritage of African Americans and explored the complexities of the black experience in America. Ellington's success as a musician and bandleader also contributed to greater economic empowerment and social mobility for African American artists. He was one of the first African American musicians to achieve widespread fame and financial success in the music industry, paving the way for future generations of black performers and helping to break down racial barriers in the entertainment world. While Ellington's contributions to black justice, equality, and freedom were primarily cultural rather than political, his impact on the music industry and popular culture helped to challenge racial stereotypes and promote greater understanding and appreciation of African American art and expression. His legacy as a pioneering jazz composer and bandleader continues to inspire musicians and audiences around the world, and his music remains a powerful testament to the creativity, resilience, and cultural richness of the African American experience.

In the rhythm of life, there danced a Duke,
With melodies smooth, and a piano he'd pluck.
Composer, bandleader, a legend in jazz,
His music would make even the stiffest toes tap.

Duke Ellington, a maestro of sound,
With each note he played, a story he'd expound.
From smoky clubs to grand concert halls,
His music transcended, breaking down walls.

But what if Duke were here with us now?
How would he jazz up the world, somehow?
Perhaps he'd be grooving on YouTube live,
Or hosting a podcast where stories thrive.

In a world of streaming and digital beats,
He'd remind us all of the joy that repeats.
With a twinkle in his eye and a swing in his step,
He'd inspire men to create without misstep.

So, men of today, take heed and embrace,
The spirit of Duke, in every space.
In honoring his legacy, we find our own grace,
And make Black men proud, in every place.

So, raise a glass to Duke, his music divine,
And may we all let our creativity shine.
For in his rhythms, we find our way,
To a brighter tomorrow, come what may!

Aretha Franklin (1942 – 2018) was a legendary African American singer, songwriter, and civil rights activist who made profound contributions to music and fought for black justice, equality, and freedom through her artistry and activism. Franklin's most notable achievement was her unparalleled career as the "Queen of Soul." With her powerful voice, emotional depth, and unparalleled vocal range, she became one of the most influential and successful recording artists of all time. Franklin's iconic hits, including "Respect," "Chain of Fools," and "Think," not only topped the charts but also became anthems of empowerment and social change. Through her music, Franklin addressed themes of empowerment, love, and social justice, providing a voice for the African American community and challenging racial discrimination and inequality. Her rendition of "Respect" became an anthem for both the civil rights and women's rights movements, encapsulating the demand for dignity, equality, and respect. In addition to her musical achievements, Franklin was also a vocal advocate for civil rights and social justice. She supported the civil rights movement and performed at numerous benefit concerts and rallies in support of racial equality and justice. Her activism extended beyond her performances, as she used her platform to speak out against injustice and inequality. Franklin's impact on the music industry and popular culture helped to challenge racial stereotypes and promote greater understanding and appreciation of African American art and expression. She was the first woman to be inducted into the Rock and Roll Hall of Fame and received numerous awards and honors throughout her career, including the Presidential Medal of Freedom. Aretha Franklin's legacy as a pioneering musician and civil rights activist continues to inspire generations of artists and activists around the world. Her music remains a powerful testament to the resilience, strength, and beauty of the African American experience, and her commitment to fighting for black justice, equality, and freedom serves as a beacon of hope and inspiration for social change.

In the realm of music, she reigns supreme,
Aretha Franklin, the Queen of Soul's dream.
With a voice so potent, it could move the stars,
She belted out tunes from deep within her heart.

Oh, imagine now, if she were still around,
With her soulful croon, she'd astound.
Perhaps she'd be sipping tea with the stars,
Trading tales with legends on Jupiter or Mars.

But here on Earth, her legacy lives on strong,
In every note of her timeless songs.
She taught us to sing with passion and grace,
To wear our crowns proudly, no need to race.

For women today, she's a beacon of light,
Showing us how to stand tall and fight.
To embrace our power, to own our sound,
And let our voices echo, unbounded and unbound.

So, let's raise a glass to the Queen of Soul,
Her spirit is forever in our heart's bowl.
May we carry her torch, shine bright and bold,
And make our sisters proud, as she once told.

Kendrick Lamar (born June 17, 1987) is an influential African American rapper, songwriter, and record producer whose music explores themes of black identity, social justice, and inequality. Through his artistry and activism, Lamar has made significant contributions to the fight for black justice, equality, and freedom. Lamar's most notable achievement is his groundbreaking music career. With critically acclaimed albums such as "good kid, m.A.A.d City," "To Pimp a Butterfly," and "DAMN.," he has earned widespread acclaim for his lyricism, storytelling, and social commentary. Lamar's music often addresses issues such as police brutality, systemic racism, and the struggles faced by African Americans in inner-city communities. Through his music, Lamar has become a voice for marginalized communities, advocating for social change and justice. His album "To Pimp a Butterfly," in particular, was praised for its exploration of black identity and empowerment, earning Lamar multiple Grammy Awards and widespread recognition as one of the most influential albums of the 21st century. In addition to his musical achievements, Lamar has been actively involved in social and political activism. He has spoken out against racial injustice and inequality, participated in protests and marches, and used his platform to raise awareness about issues affecting African Americans. In 2018, Lamar won the Pulitzer Prize for Music for "DAMN.," becoming the first non-classical or jazz artist to receive the honor. Lamar's impact on the music industry and popular culture has helped to challenge stereotypes and promote greater understanding and appreciation of African American experiences. His commitment to fighting for black justice, equality, and freedom continues to inspire fans and activists around the world, and his legacy as a pioneering artist and activist will undoubtedly leave a lasting impact on generations to come.

Aubrey Drake Graham, known professionally as Drake, is a Canadian rapper, singer, songwriter, actor, and entrepreneur. While he hasn't been extensively involved in explicit activism, Drake's achievements and influence have contributed to broader conversations about black justice, equality, and freedom. Drake's most notable achievement is his immense success in the music industry. He has released several critically acclaimed albums, including "Take Care," "Nothing Was the Same," and "Views," which have all topped charts and received numerous awards. Drake's versatile style, catchy melodies, and introspective lyrics have earned him a massive global fanbase and solidified his status as one of the most influential artists of his generation. As one of the most prominent black artists in mainstream music, Drake has used his platform to amplify the voices of black artists and creators. He has collaborated with numerous black artists across various genres, helping to elevate their careers and bring attention to their work. Additionally, Drake has been vocal about issues affecting the black community in his music, addressing themes such as racial injustice, poverty, and the challenges faced by marginalized communities. Beyond his music career, Drake has also ventured into entrepreneurship, with successful business ventures in fashion, alcohol, and sports. He has used his wealth and influence to support various charitable causes, including initiatives aimed at supporting black youth and promoting education and social justice. While Drake's contributions to black justice, equality, and freedom may not be as overt as some other artists, his success and visibility as a black artist in the music industry have undoubtedly helped to challenge stereotypes and promote greater representation and diversity in mainstream media. His influence as a cultural icon continues to resonate with audiences worldwide, and his legacy as a pioneering artist and entrepreneur will likely continue to inspire future generations.

In the world of hip-hop, where beats and rhymes
collide,
Two giants stand tall, with talent as their guide.
Kendrick Lamar and Aubrey Graham, names that
resound,
In the heart of the genre, where greatness is found.

Kendrick, with his words like a razor's edge,
Carving truth and wisdom on every lyrical pledge.
His social commentary, sharp and profound,
Echoes through minds, a powerful sound.

And then there's Aubrey, smooth as silk,
Blending rap with R&B, like fine-crafted milk.
His melodies soar, his flow so sweet,
In the world of hip-hop, he takes a front seat.

Their paths may cross, their styles may differ,
But in their essence, they both shimmer.
Addressing fame, struggle, societal strife,
Each carving their niche, defining their life.

Yet amidst their brilliance, a tension may brew,
A competitive spirit, pushing them anew.
But let's pause for a moment, and imagine a scene,
Where rivalry fades, and peace reigns supreme.

They could collaborate, blend their unique styles,
Creating magic that stretches for miles.
Inspiring young artists, breaking down walls,
Showing the world, unity never falls.

So, to the young black men, looking for stars to follow,
Kendrick and Aubrey, in them find no sorrow.
For in their journeys, in their highs and their lows,
They teach us to rise, to conquer our woes.

Let's celebrate their greatness, their impact profound,
And in their unity, let harmony resound.
For Kendrick Lamar and Aubrey Graham, in their own right,
Illuminate the path, shining ever so bright.

AFTERWORD

Other black intellectuals, freedom fighters, civil rights leaders, and artists such as Nat King Cole, Ray Charles, Sam Cooke, Mahalia Jackson, Little Richard, Chuck Berry, Etta James, Dinah Washington, Sarah Vaughan, Fats Domino, Marvin Gaye, James Brown, Diana Ross (with The Supremes), Stevie Wonder, Otis Redding, Smokey Robinson, Wilson Pickett, Gladys Knight (with The Pips), Curtis Mayfield, Al Green, Tina Turner, Donna Summer, Isaac Hayes, Sly Stone (with Sly and the Family Stone), Bill Withers, Roberta Flack, The Temptations, The Isley Brothers, and Gladys Knight, among many others, have all made significant contributions in paving the way for future generations of African Americans, shaping the landscape of American culture in music, intellectual curiosity, social justice, and innovations in art, science, and technology, for years to come.

As we come to the close of this collection of poems, it is imperative to reflect on the profound influence of our ancestors and the pioneers of the civil rights movement on the landscape of today's black youth. From the harrowing tales of African slave freedom fighters to the courageous strides of civil rights activists, their legacies serve as beacons of hope and inspiration in the face of adversity.

Despite the victories won and the freedoms fought for, our youth still find themselves navigating treacherous waters, grappling with the harsh realities of a world fraught with peril. The echoes of past rap battles that turned deadly, like those of Christopher Wallace and Tupac Amaru Shakur, still reverberate, serving as stark reminders of the consequences of aimless conflict.

Even now, as Kendrick Lamar and Aubrey Graham find themselves embroiled in a rap battle with potentially deadly consequences, it is crucial for today's youth to heed the lessons of the past. The sacrifices made by freedom fighters like Frederick Douglas, Harriet Tubman, Martin Luther King, Malcolm X, Rosa Parks, John Lewis, Medgar Evers, and countless others must not be in vain.

In the face of the legacy of slavery, racism, and inequality that still plagues our society, it is paramount that the youth of today draw strength from the resilience and courage of those who came before. Let us strive to live lives of peace, productivity, and purpose, honoring the sacrifices made and paving the way for a brighter future for generations to come.

In conclusion, as we turn the final page of this book, may these poems serve as a reminder of the power of perseverance, the importance of unity, and the enduring legacy of hope. Let us march forward, guided by the spirits of our ancestors, towards a tomorrow where justice, equality, and love reign supreme.

The End